THE PHENOMENOLOGY OF PREGNANCY AND EARLY MOTHERHOOD

The Phenomenology of Pregnancy and Early Motherhood provides an ethical, social and psychological investigation of the process of becoming a mother.

Through a phenomenological analysis that engages with feminist philosophy, medical ethics, philosophy of care and phenomenological psychology, Susi Ferrarello unravels the intricacies of this transformative phase of life to shed light on layers of lived experiences that impact the well-being of the woman. This book addresses the complexity of common lived experiences characterizing this transition: the overarching period from the first to the fourth trimester, issues concerning maternal–fetal bonding, breastfeeding, perinatal mood and anxiety disorders, loss of identity and coming back to work. Enriched by case studies from Ferrarello's philosophical counseling practice, the book provides a compassionate and insightful exploration of the struggles, triumphs and moments of self-revelation that mothers encounter in their daily lives. By exploring the heart of the maternal experience, this book shows the often-unspoken realities faced by women as they strive to balance their roles as caregivers, partners and individuals. The book offers a powerful means for everyday reflection on early motherhood and the ethical, as well as practical, dilemmas it raises.

This text is an essential resource for graduate students studying phenomenology, ethics, feminist philosophy and moral psychology, as well as therapists and professionals interested in the challenges of pregnancy, motherhood and women's mental health.

Susi Ferrarello, Ph.D., is an associate professor at California State University, East Bay. She works as a philosophical counselor and also writes for *Psychology Today*.

THE PHENOMENOLOGY OF PREGNANCY AND EARLY MOTHERHOOD

Ethical, Social, and Psychological Perspectives

Susi Ferrarello

Routledge
Taylor & Francis Group

NEW YORK AND LONDON

Designed cover image: Getty Images

First published 2025
by Routledge
605 Third Avenue, New York, NY 10158

and by Routledge
4 Park Square, Milton Park, Abingdon, Oxon, OX14 4RN

*Routledge is an imprint of the Taylor & Francis Group, an informa
business*

ISBN: 978-1-032-78631-5 (hbk)
ISBN: 978-1-032-79196-8 (pbk)
ISBN: 978-1-003-49093-7 (ebk)

DOI: 10.4324/9781003490937

Typeset in Times New Roman
by Apex CoVantage, LLC

Al mio piccolo, León.

CONTENTS

INTRODUCTION

As I completed writing this book, I received very bad news: a school friend of mine had committed suicide, leaving behind her two children. The reasons for her choice were not clear to her family and closest friends. She was a beautiful, healthy woman who managed to be caring toward friends and family but maybe not herself. This event reminded me that, within my small circle of friends, she was not the only woman to commit suicide. Three other women, from different social statuses and lifestyles, also made this choice. All of them were mothers, and all left at least two children behind.

As I conclude this book and write this introduction, I still wonder if there is a way to help improve the quality of life for women, particularly mothers. One phenomenon I noticed but did not have time to investigate here is the progressive medicalization of women who have more than one child. I observed that women who experience exhaustion tend to embark on the endless chain of duties that motherhood demands until they reach a point of no return, often resulting in chronic disease or serious illness. This gives them "an excuse" in front of their harshest judge—themselves—to lessen their family workload and focus on their own needs. Should we really wait for this to happen before giving the right attention to the quality of life of new mothers?

Transformations

In a recent article, Berg (2024) critiques the concept of transformation in motherhood, arguing that women do not always undergo significant changes when they become mothers. This perspective resonated with me due to a distinct experience I had when my child was 3 months old. My husband came home early to allow me to attend a faculty meeting online. The two and a half hours of the meeting passed pleasantly, with smooth discussions and no stressful agenda items. However, I distinctly recall experiencing a strong sense of identity confusion when the meeting ended. The person attending the meeting felt like my usual self, who had not gone through labor and three months of sleepless nights. Yet, as the meeting concluded and I returned to my child, I felt almost guilty for the pleasure I took in reconnecting with that familiar, pre-motherhood self, even if only for a moment.

This experience aligns with Berg's criticism of the notion of transformation in early motherhood. However, I believe that even if a complete transformation does not occur (we do not necessarily change our bodily shape or acquire a new identity), parts of us transform and a unique identity experience takes place. Phenomenologically speaking, Berg continues, "[W]hen I try to focus on this experience, it feels a little like trying to focus on the transparency of the air. . . . It is not grand and tremendous. It is not even extraordinary" (2024, p. 1). She uses philosopher Agnes Callard's reflection on the relief following an unplanned pregnancy loss to describe childbirth as "literally, splitting in two, and you don't know which one your I goes with" (Callard, 2020).

I understand the feeling of being split during pregnancy and early motherhood. However, in this book, I defend the concept of embodied intersubjectivity against notions of alienation and feeling split. I argue that these notions can better serve us in understanding ourselves as a *continuum* with the transformation that is taking place, similar to a tree whose roots and branches grow deeper and spread wider. The tree remains the same while changing at the same time. While Berg presents a compelling case against transformation, her description of women feeling split into multiple new identities can also be interpreted as a form of transformation—where the old self adapts to caring for a new baby within a new lifestyle.

I believe that the idea of embodied intersubjectivity better explains the stretching that women undergo as they become mothers while still being the women they were. Splitting reinforces the sense of fragmentation that might emphasize despair without explaining why we keep feeling somehow still ourselves in the storm.

Rachel Bertsche, in her 2020 *New York Times* article titled "When Your Name Becomes 'Mom,' Do Your Other Identities Matter?" expresses nostalgia for her pre-parenthood identity, mourning the spontaneity and freedom she once enjoyed (Bertsche, 2020). Sheila Heti, in her book "Motherhood", highlights the isolating aspect of motherhood, noting how a parent's focus shifts predominantly toward the child, often sidelining other aspects of identity (Heti, 2018). These reflections underscore the complex and often underappreciated phenomenological reality of becoming a mother.

In this book, I challenge Berg's idea that motherhood is not phenomenologically interesting; otherwise, this book would not have been written. Understanding the identity shift that occurs in early motherhood can help improve the quality of life for women who might feel lost during this transformative experience.

Structure of the Book

When I presented parts of this book at a conference attended by colleagues from various fields—philosophy, psychiatry, social work, anthropology and others— my observations were positively received. More importantly, these scholars approached me afterward as concerned human beings. Fathers worried about the well-being of their daughters, who were new mothers; husbands strived to support their wives lost in the fog of motherhood and sisters tried to be the village their siblings needed. No new mothers were present, of course, as they were too busy taking care of their babies. This is my fear. This book, aimed at improving the well-being of new mothers, might not reach them directly because they are too busy caring for their families. Moreover, once they rejoin life as they knew it, or a version of it, many will try to forget the hardships and retain only the good memories. This is why I wrote this book while I was in the thick of it—to capture the complexity of this delicate lived experience that affects us all but seems to burden only a few. We need to gain a deeper understanding of what it means to become a mother to improve the quality of life for the women who contribute significantly to the progress of society. Motherhood is not a whim but a fundamental aspect of our humanity. As humans, we should learn how to make space for each other in our society.

The chapters are organized as follows. The first chapter introduces readers to narratives of pregnancy and motherhood, exploring the psychological and phenomenological journey of women transitioning from pregnancy to early motherhood. Using the metaphor "sealskin, soulskin", it addresses themes of identity loss, isolation and transformation. Inspired by observing mothers in family photographs, I investigate the emotional shifts accompanying motherhood, framing the discussion within a Husserlian perspective on time. The narrative critiques simplistic depictions of motherhood, emphasizing the importance of reconnecting with personal skills and resources to regain a sense of wholeness. Through dialogue with diverse personal stories, the chapter highlights the visceral, embodied experiences of new mothers and challenges societal expectations. By weaving together individual narratives, this chapter aims to mend fragmented experiences, offering a space for shared understanding and solidarity.

The second chapter, "No Bump, No Care", presents three core problems that might appear in the first trimester of pregnancy: alienation, objectification and loss of identity, which can cause emotional distress and potentially develop into depressive states. The chapter outlines a mindful approach to mitigate these issues. For alienation, it suggests that mindful presence should be paid to the construction of new habitualities, allowing women to connect with their primor-dial impulses and build a consistent core of pre-reflective habits. For objectifica-tion, it advises women to pay mindful attention to the daily interplay between Leib (living body) and Koerper (physical body), exploring the new range of possibilities. For loss of identity, it stresses the importance of attending to vital feelings to maintain a sense of self-worth and identity. The chapter advocates for addressing emotional problems from the first trimester rather than exclu-sively post-partum.

The third chapter focuses on breastfeeding, framing it as an embodied lived experience. Despite being treated as a disembodied, intellectual activity, breast-feeding is an intimate, full-time job that fosters bonding between mother and child. This chapter explores how breastfeeding guidelines often ignore the per-sonal and embodied nature of the practice, sidelining women from their own expertise. It uses phenomenological notions of life-world, agency and autono-mous choice to examine the impact on mothers' psychological well-being.

The fourth chapter discusses volitions and motivations during pregnancy and early motherhood, examining how volitions are driven by primal forces rather than subjectivity. It highlights the importance of small actions in reinforcing motivational forces and fostering a renewed identity. The chapter emphasizes the mystery of life and the ongoing transformation involved in motherhood.

The fifth chapter was supposed to address technology's impact on women's intimate lives before and after pregnancy. Unfortunately, because of space, because the book grew more than I expected in the proposal, I had to cut it.

Hence, the fifth chapter reflects on the transformative process of transition-ing from pregnancy to motherhood, emphasizing that this transformation begins even before pregnancy. It explores how pregnancy fosters embodied intersubjec-tivity, leading to a new form of empathetic connection with the baby. The chapter argues for an immanent self-transcendence where women overcome their limits while staying within them, highlighting steps such as witnessing blood, enduring pain and trusting their growing bodies.

The final chapter examines the psychological intricacies of childbirth and the journey back to oneself. Using the "sealskin, soulskin" metaphor, it explores themes of death and femicide in this transformative process. The chapter empha-sizes the importance of reconnecting with skills and resources within one's own space and time, demonstrating that the constitutive notion of time after delivery is that of a living present. It discusses how visceral needs and intersubjective instincts shape the woman's experience, stressing the importance of reclaiming one's skills and resources to truly come back to oneself.

The chapters aim to fill gaps in the literature regarding the first and fourth trimesters, providing a mirror to reflect on moments of the lived experience of becoming a mother.

References

Berg, A. (2024, June 11). What if motherhood isn't transformative at all? *The Cut*. https://www.thecut.com/article/excerpt-what-are-children-for-anastasia-berg.html?fbclid=IwZXh0bgNhZW0CMTEAAR3FAUfHyDPns2bYmfVnJBjcQZxbN-fNtTOb0srTXU9kIU336eyfw4XVtEM_aem_ZmFrZWR1bW15MTZieXRlcw

Bertsche, R. (2020). When your name becomes mum. *The New York Times*. https://www.nytimes.com/2020/04/16/parenting/motherhood-identity-crisis.html

Callard, A. (2020). Parenting and panic. *The Point*. https://thepointmag.com/examined-life/parenting-and-panic-agnes-callard/

Heti, S. (2018). *Motherhood*. Henry Holt and Co.

1

WEAVE AND MEND

Stories of Pregnancy and Motherhood

> She is a fierce spirit: A dangerous woman, and anyone who crosses her will
> not easily sing a song of triumph. But here come the boys after their run, sus-
> pecting nothing of their mother's tragedy. She frightens me.
>
> Euripides, Medea, trans. Paul Roche, lines 50–56

I. Women Who Come Back

The original title I chose for this book was "Women Who Come Back", but
my editor strongly advised against it. The cover—because we do judge a book
by its cover—would have been too vague in respect to the book's content. It
was more prudent to be explicit in the title about my approach, phenomenology
and focus on my study: pregnant women transitioning from pregnancy to early
motherhood.

Nevertheless, this remains, for me, a book about women who have found their
way back to themselves and their lives. Through these pages, I did not intend
to speak on behalf of all women—that would be impossible. However, I hope
to encapsulate the experiences of at least some, as the journey of becoming
a mother needs to be told in both its light and shadows. Therefore, this chapter features stories from diverse individuals—men and women, cisgender and
non-cisgender—of various ages and from different parts of the world, sharing
their perspectives on what "motherhood" means to them. In the subsequent chapters, I establish a thematic and conceptual dialogue with these stories to articulate
what this experience entails in one's life.

The inspiration for this book came from photo albums of baptisms, first birth-
days and early memories of young children. I noticed that if a relative or friend

DOI: 10.4324/9781003490937-1

paid closer attention to the faces in these pictures, they would see how the mothers appeared somehow distant from everyone else around them, even from the ground beneath their feet. Their eyes seemed to be somewhere else—far away. These are the women I want to honor in this book. I want to understand where they went when they looked so remote, whether they ever came back and, if they did, whether they felt different.

In these pages, I reflect on how pregnancy and early motherhood appear when everything goes well—when you have a healthy baby you deeply desire with the husband you love. Even then, as I have come to understand, happiness and isolation often seem to be two sides of the same coin. In the chapters, I explore the sense of loss, disorientation and absence that many mothers (not necessarily first-time mothers) experience as they struggle to fit into this new role. Losing one's identity, as it often happens in this transformation, might be a blessing in disguise as it allows one to come in contact with resources previously unknown. Becoming a mother is a profound inner journey for women (and not limited to them); where this journey leads and what they become remains unknown. However, it is a transformation that we can observe, reflect upon and seek to understand (Bergum, 1986, p. 67).

II. Weave and Mend

> I am scattered/There are women everywhere with fragments/gather fragments/weave and mend/When we learn to come together we are whole.
>
> (Cameron, 1981, p. 149)[1]

"Weave and mend"—weaving stories mends wounds. In sharing some of our stories, we come together, intertwining in a whole that is both personal and intersubjective. The word "mother" is a whole in which many different women learn to recognize themselves, even though each merges into it with her own name. We teach our children, "I am your mom". But this "I" serves an inscrutable whole—the mother whose role is the same for everyone. How we become this whole is an individual journey that we share with each other.

As I noted in Chapter 5, hopefully the stories we tell each other are more like gossip than serious ethical tirades. There is nothing official or definitive about looking back reflectively; rather, each story is a moment of intimate truth that unexpectedly reveals itself to other women we may not know well but with whom we feel an affinity in the moment.

For this reason, attempting to write something definitive about pregnancy and motherhood is almost impossible, if not pointless. The array of experiences is so vast that it inevitably feels biased to choose one story over another. Even words are insufficient to capture the complexity of this experience. Should we call the woman a mother in a world where surrogates, gender-fluid individuals, adoptive parents and polyamorous clusters experience motherhood in very different ways? Should I instead use the term "primary caregiver"? But then, who is really a primary caregiver? Does it even make sense to differentiate between primary and secondary caregivers, especially in families where both parents work full-time? What qualifies someone as the primary caregiver—the one who earns less?

Motherhood is a choice that occurs separately from the act of giving birth. As I will discuss in Chapter 5, becoming a mother involves a series of habituations and bodily schemas that do not necessarily align with our traditional binary way of organizing parenthood, where a mother generates the child and a father provides for their livelihood. Since the right words are lacking, I have chosen to stick with traditional terms, keeping them as open as possible to encompass the wide variety of nuances in which we can experience "motherhood" today and in the years to come.

In talking to people and collecting stories for this book, I heard about mothers who were emotionally absent because they were too involved in their careers or too withdrawn in their emotional wounds, unable to muster the energy to get out of bed and leave their rooms. Their daughters and sons shared their stories with me, "weaving and mending" in bits and pieces, trying to become whole in a society that has prescribed a very specific set of behaviors for them.

Why did the emotionally absent mother cause more pain than the completely absent father? One participant told me that as he was growing up, his aunt always advised him not to bother his mom when she was in her room because she was mentally too weak to spend time with him. Why was a depressed mom left alone to take care of her son? In this case, I know that the mother had been forced to give up her job because it was deemed partly inappropriate for a woman to work instead of dedicating her full-time to taking care of her child, and her salary was not as good as her husband's. She was not mentally weak; she felt purposeless and robbed of her talent, working for a household that probably felt too confining. Sometimes the primary caregiver does not have a choice because the secondary caregiver—more often a man—is not assigned the same responsibilities that society has tailored around her. Unfortunately, we do not know if she ever got to tell her story because she may never have found her way back to a sense of wholeness.

Many women who initially responded to my invitation enthusiastically later stepped back, sometimes just hours after agreeing, because they realized how challenging the task would be; the process might bring them back to a place where they felt scattered. "I have been through so much that I do not want to relive it again", one woman told me over the phone. Another wrote, "I would love to, but I simply do not have time to sit and write with my children around and a life to keep going".

Being able to come together, weave, mend and become whole is a challenging task that I hope to facilitate with this book.

III. Living the Question

Over the past two years, this book has been both a refuge where I could reconnect with myself (or at least demonstrate commitment to the task) and an exhausting goal that confronted me with the complexity of my experiences. As Timpe (2023) notes, engaging in philosophical work as an act of care can entail emotional burdens due to unique aspects inherent in such projects, extending beyond the conventional academic framework. These endeavors, aimed at philosophical care, may exact a toll on those involved. However, it is within this commitment to care that we cultivate a deeply human exploration, delving into the varied dimensions of our existence. While writing this book, I grappled with both existential and academic questions simultaneously—where am I? Am I coming back? Can others see me?

Reflecting on these questions led my research to explore lived experiences that, while categorized similarly to mine, were fundamentally different in many ways. This added not only an additional layer of emotional fatigue but also personal enrichment, as I became acquainted with a submerged universe I would not have encountered had I not decided to write this book. Knowing this, I realized I could not speak for every woman, but I could at least give voice to the lived experiences of some. What I found common in many stories was a sense of invisibility. It was easy for friends and relatives to overlook the profound changes that can revolutionize a woman's role after pregnancy and early motherhood. In my own case, when interacting with people who used to know me well, I often thought that sooner or later they would realize it was not truly me talking to them. They would see that someone else was speaking, while the real me was, so to speak, submerged beneath light-green water, floating alongside aquatic vegetation.

Realizing this connected me to my sense of guilt toward all the women—friends, students, colleagues and relatives—who became mothers before me. I did not understand the magnitude of the transition they were undergoing. I approached their journey into motherhood as if they were merely adjusting to a new job they had eagerly desired or settling into a new home purchased after signing a steep mortgage. Now, I recognize that the significance of such an event is comparable to a metaphorical death, given the profound psychological and physical transformation it entails.

In the following stories, as well as in the book, death is among the themes I explore. Soon after giving birth, I dreamt about my death in various ways. This was not due to depression; I was quite happy and in love with my newborn. Yet, despite my immense joy for the new life, I experienced a sense of impending death several times. The first time I left for a conference, I feared I would not return to him. The most pronounced feeling of death occurred six months after his birth when a very close friend visited for a few days. I remember spending a good part of that time thinking that if I died, she would be a perfect replacement for me. In my mind, I believed that life had given me too much and it was time for me to go; alternatively, I felt I no longer existed for anyone, so it would be better for me to leave. In both scenarios, I remember thinking that someone would eventually realize that it was not truly me there, and this impostor should be discovered and asked to leave. By then, my dear friend, the replacement, would have perfectly fit into the new household.

This was just one of the many remote thoughts that occupied the back of my mind as I juggled learning so many new things about myself, my child and my work. As I discovered through writing the book, similar thoughts seem to have occurred in many other women as well. Hence, to address the question—how can I articulate all these thoughts that mark the transition to motherhood? How can I give substance to all these layers we shed as we grow into the role of motherhood? In this book, I decided to engage in dialogue with some of the lived experiences of the women who responded to my invitation to discuss some major milestones characterizing this transition: the first trimester, breastfeeding, the role of media and technology, how we change and how we find our way back.

IV. Stories

Sometimes a story might ensnare us. Confining pregnancy and motherhood to just one narrative would be erroneous. It is not possible to write a definitive story about any major life event. The same story is, in fact, many stories that we revisit repeatedly with our bodies; each time something is different. The event remains equally true in each of these stories, but the way in which we remember and relate to it changes every time. Reducing women's stories to clinical terms prevents the unfolding of what childbirth and motherhood truly entail.

Narratives might become a trap (Dolan & Henwood, 2021). The use of grammar, time and narrative rules constrains the story within a space that cannot reflect what we actually lived when we try to make sense of life-altering events. Every story has the right to instability. Especially in this revolution, we owe ourselves the time to be awkward, to forget the words, to get lost in our thoughts and to feel overwhelmed because we are learning. We are learning about one of the most phenomenal events that can happen in one's life—coming to life.

Hence, the stories below come mostly from women I was in dialogue with before and after writing this book. Unfortunately, the constraints of publishing oblige us to document just one of the many possible ways in which the person might have told their stories. In the chapters, I honored the variables that each story might encounter.

The participants come from different sexes, ages, nationalities and countries; even the time frame varies. Some of them wrote their stories ten years after their experiences. I tried to be as inclusive as possible to avoid featuring only Western, white or female cisgender voices. Some stories have been translated into English by me, as they were originally in German or French. These words, although provisional tokens of a kaleidoscopic experience, have been important references for confronting my own experience and initiating a comprehensive dialogue with myself that informed the research in this book. I am very grateful for the time they spent trying to capture at least a fragment of their own stories.

IV.1   Maternity and Pregnancy[2]

> *Marzia is a 48-year-old woman living in northern Europe but originally from a Mediterranean country. She is telling her story while fully in it since her younger child is still in daycare. She responded very quickly to my invitation. I translated her words from Italian into English.*

Maternity, in my view, begins before conception, at the moment when one feels ready to become a mother and starts to envision oneself in that role. Pregnancy, on the other hand, is a physical experience that belongs to the body, which during pregnancy no longer feels entirely one's own.

The desire to conceive and the anticipation of pregnancy are accompanied by varying degrees of anxiety. Experiences of miscarriage can exacerbate these feelings, intensifying the sense of failure as a woman perpetuated by societal and familial expectations. When I disclosed my miscarriage at eight weeks to my mother, she suggested that I might be somehow broken. Such responses, though hurtful, intensified my pervasive feeling of inadequacy in procreation.

I have encountered many women who have gone through miscarriages, ectopic pregnancies and stillbirths, and we all felt somewhat broken, with deep emotional wounds. My first pregnancy with Marco was complicated; at the morphological scan, we discovered that Marco had a heart defect, leading to a tumultuous journey through the highs and lows of parenthood, medical interventions and, ultimately, loss.

After Marco's passing, I sought therapy to confront my grief and fears, allowing myself to mourn his loss and release him. Therapy helped me navigate through the pain, and soon after, I became pregnant again. Despite facing severe morning sickness for six months, I found solace in the care of my gynecologist and the support of my community. Leonardo was born a day before the scheduled cesarean section, bringing tears of relief and joy.

Motherhood, despite its challenges, has been a remarkable journey of self-discovery and love. Marco taught me how to love, Leonardo has loved me unconditionally and Andrea tests me with his strong personality, constantly pushing me to question and grow as a mother.

IV.2 Early Motherhood—Patricia

> Patricia is in her early fifties from northern America. She raised her children in a country different from where she was originally born without the support of her family or friends. She recounts her experience while she has been dealing with the parenting challenges that her now adolescent kid brings to her and her husband.

I stood in the living room with a martini in one hand and the urine test stick in the other. I was aghast. I was only taking the pregnancy test because my period was late, and I thought I should check before scheduling an appointment with my doctor to see what was going on with my cycle; it never crossed my mind that I could actually be pregnant. The martini became a symbol of my clear shock—I wouldn't have been drinking if I thought there was even a slim chance that I could be pregnant. And I was. I was 33 and had just gotten engaged to be married a month earlier. We had discussed that we wanted children sometime, but ideally this would be in a few years. I didn't feel ready at all and very much wanted to be engaged and married and enjoy that for a while before introducing a child into the mix. But at the same time, it didn't feel right to abort a baby that we would eventually want, particularly given how challenging it can be for some people to get pregnant. I dumped the martini down the sink and told my fiancé, now husband, that we were having a child.

At first, his excitement and clear welcoming of this baby are what made it possible for me to embrace what was happening even a little bit. It also made it possible for me to handle all that was needed to change in my life and in my body, none of which felt comfortable or easy. I was feeling completely overwhelmed and taken over by the experience on every front. I had a consulting job that required me to travel, and that week alone I flew to three different cities. A few weeks later the morning sickness came, and I felt very vulnerable on planes and could no longer offer good excuses for not being able to participate in late sales dinners with clients. The slight smell of wine (or raw meat, or cigarettes, or gasoline or certain people or foods) made me very nauseous. And I was always hungry and always so so so deeply exhausted. In a matter of two months, my usual rational, capable, overachieving self was so distant. I ate, slept and emoted, often irrationally, as if I were having PMS but on steroids. With the small amount of energy I had left, I started looking for a new job—one without travel—and I did not tell them I was pregnant out of fear that they might not hire me if they knew. My body became unfamiliar and bloated and heavy, and I could no longer wear anything and didn't yet have a sense of maternity fashion. I felt immediately old, frumpy and fat.

The second and third trimesters were much better because I didn't feel so shocked or confused, and I was sufficiently naïve about babies to be able to tell myself that it would be easy. Other people congratulated me and told me this was a wonderful thing. I wasn't so sure but gave into the experience. Sure, I had babysat before and taught kids swimming lessons, but I didn't really know much about breastfeeding or birth. I told myself I wouldn't become one of those boring moms who never go out anymore and who wear boring clothing and so on. I would still do interesting things and think deeply and express myself. How little I understood about what was about to occur. Couldn't I take my newborn everywhere with me? Stay out late and do the same things I did before? What was the big deal?!

My water broke three weeks early, and I carried the strep B virus, so I was admitted and induced into labor. All the birthing classes and birth planning we had done was now out of our hands as my body and the little body of my daughter did what they had in mind. I labored for four days with Pitocin and finally got a C-section. I never dilated fully. She was so small. And so sweet and so utterly precious, but the realities of nursing, which I could do well, were so hard. I woke up every 90 minutes or two hours around the clock at first to feed her and to keep my milk flowing. For the next year, she screamed with colic as she had a bad case of GERD and often experienced pain. After many trips to the doctor and many nights sleeping upright with her in my arms (Sleeping upright helped her to not feel the reflux and thus she would not scream in pain.) and after her esophagus matured more, she began to sleep through the night. It wasn't until she was 2 that I was able to go back to work in earnest. The first years I worked a few hours here and there and tried to get a shower or a nap in between. We staggered through the days, and any ideas about my old life—seeing movies in a theater, going to concerts or dinners or wearing nice clothing that didn't smell of spit up—were distant. She was lovely and easy after that, but in the process I had lost any real connection to my former self.

I would spend my days walking with her and friends who had infants, going to mommy and me groups or Gymboree or music classes and doing my work when the nanny came. Sex was planned, if it happened at all, during her naps, and once in a while we would go on date night. Everything was scheduled in little boxes of time between her naps and feedings and the nanny and work. Nothing spontaneous at all, and it all functioned best if I just accommodated everyone's needs. We didn't have a ton of money, and the grandparents were either too old or too far away to be of much help. If I wanted to sleep in or eat late or not stop at the park or talk for a while with a friend or whatever, I would be penalized by crying and whining, which was hard to tolerate. *Children find a way to get their needs met, and it felt to me like a mainline into my heart.* So I put myself aside in many ways for years.

People were not so into MILF porn then, and there wasn't as much marketing and gadgets and parenting advice then. In some ways that is nice because we got to raise our children without the torment of content and products telling us we were doing it wrong or the pressure to have it all by being sexy and a mother. Our daughter went to preschool and then elementary school, and we had another child along the way. What I think I have realized is that to become a mother is a process that occurs on the bodily and emotional level. Mothers put their needs and personalities aside and allow themselves to be used and influenced in a bodily way. It is very animalistic and primal. And I think it is for the benefit of the species ultimately, but it is an abrupt and intense change—at least it was for me. As they age, there are other ways that the whole process is humbling. Children are who they are, and we can see the seeds of who they are now in who they were as infants. We have an impact on how they turn out, but their fundamental temperaments and drives can't be shaped much. There is a lot of awe in this. They are whole separate people who are developing, and we have to often stand aside and put our values, beliefs or preferences aside and allow this development to occur. This is most prevalent in adolescence, where children need to push against us to define themselves. This is so that they get out from under the protective wing (of the mother) so they can learn to fly, but that process combined with hormones (and in our case, menopause too) is not so elegant and kind. The older child must hate and push against its mother (and father) in order to launch and define herself. It's awful and wonderful in equal doses. Somehow becoming a mother is the most meaningful thing in the world. It is important and facilitates understanding of oneself and others, unlike anything else. But for me, it took a huge toll on my freedom and will take time to develop again when the children leave. And we mother to provide children with all that they need so that they can parent others to do the same.

IV.3 Transition From Pregnancy to Motherhood—Camilla

Camilla is in her early twenties. She lives in North America although she is originally from a Mediterranean country. Before having a chance to truly adjust to her new life in America and the changes this involved, she had her daughter. She liked her job and her new life.

I consider myself fortunate because I had a truly beautiful pregnancy. Neither was I "victim" to morning sickness, nor did I experience any physical problems or conditions that required me to slow down my daily activities. I followed a specific training program for pregnant women that kept me fit without gaining too much weight (my belly was huge, but that's because my daughter was giant, haha). I enjoyed all the food I craved without too many worries, and I worked as long as I could (I started working part-time when I was already pregnant with my daughter).

I did have some "crisis" with my body because I was not very good at holding my urine in some situations, and this bothered me and created embarrassment for myself.

However, the more serious "problems" began after Mia was born.

The first three months were a nightmare. I lived in a state of discomfort because I didn't feel happy. It's hard to explain, but looking back now, I almost can't believe it because things have completely changed. At first, I saw Mia, but I couldn't completely rejoice in the fact that she was here. Plus, I had an unplanned cesarean section, which destabilized me a lot because of the scar that I still have difficulty seeing as something positive.

My husband even thought I had the so-called postpartum depression, and this belief made me even more upset because I was certain of what I was feeling and that it was just a momentary feeling, as it turned out to be. It may be ugly to say, but I realized that I am not a mother who would spend 24 hours a day with her daughter because I would probably end up exhausted. I need the time spent with her to be of quality, not quantity, giving myself the necessary spaces to regenerate each time. This is really important to me, and I believe my daughter will understand it too!

In general, motherhood is a beautiful wake-up call because, despite being "prepared", you can never know how it will be or what your path will be. For example, I am following a "parent coaching" program to learn the necessary tools to manage a healthy relationship and communication with my daughter.

IV.4   From Woman to a Mother

> *Kana is originally from an Asian country but living in Northern Europe. She is raising her daughter with the occasional support of her husband's family and is expecting her second daughter while writing her account. Her piece was originally written in English.*

Traditionally, a woman of my age or younger has a wish to be a mother, or we were taught to have that wish when we were girls. In Japan, it's the same; I had a natural desire to be a mother; maybe it came from my instinct, or it was an intention of the society where I belonged to, to educate girls to think like that. Anyway, I had a dream to be a mother. When I was small, I thought about what my children would look like, how they would be called and so on.

When I got over 25 years old, I started to feel a bit of pressure, maybe coming from myself because of my age, even though, unlike a typical Japanese family, my family didn't ask me when I would have children. Maybe the fact that I have endometriosis, which is known to be related to infertility, made the inner me try to hurry up and think about having children in the not far future. That is why I searched about the possibility of adopting children when I was around 30. It was not important for me to have a genetically related child, certainly because I grew up in a dysfunctional family. I never thought I wanted to leave the genetic trace of my family to the world. When I discussed adopting children with close friends, I had the impression that women are more flexible in thinking about adapting a child than men.

I got pregnant at the age of 34. I was so pleased because it was something that wouldn't happen to me because of endometriosis. During my pregnancy, I dreamed a lot about my family in Japan and the place I grew up. I "went back" to the apartment where I lived between 0 and 16 years of age, almost every night in my dreams. When I was two months pregnant, I dreamed when I was 3 years old, at five months pregnant, I was 7 years old in my dream, then at eight months pregnant, I was 10 years old in my dream and so on. I felt like I was going through my early life again. It was in chronological order. My mother was a very generous person, but she had some kind of problem ignoring the facts in front of her; for example she rarely asked what I did at school every day. She struggled a lot to decide what to prioritize in her life, career or household/growing children. She cared a lot about her social status. It was important for her that people continue considering her as "an independent working woman" even after having children. Until a very early age, like three, my mother stayed with me at home. However, after I started to go to school, she was often absent at home. Sometimes she came back home around 9 or 10 p.m. That is the reason why I wish to stay with my child as much as possible. I missed my mother at home.

Another reason why I would like to have enough time with my child is the fact that time with parents at an early age influences a lot on the mental health of the child, even after she/he becomes an adult. I prioritize my child's mental health over my career. Is there any conflict inside of me? Yes, I have honestly. I did a long education and am now working in project management at an academic publishing company. It is not what I learned for years and years: biology. Sometimes, I wonder what my education was about. To end up in this job? On the day I go to work and meet mothers/colleagues working 100% and leaving their kids to childcare and keep their position and percentage at work, the question comes to my mind. However, when I go back home and see my child's face when I stay at home with her, I am 100% sure that my choice was correct. I can say it from 100% of my heart. I am satisfied.

During my pregnancy, I was always afraid that I would be a mother who is physically present but emotionally absent. That was exactly how my mother was. Also, she was physically absent. I loved her a lot, but at the same time, I think she could be closer to me and stay with me more.

During the birth at home, I thought about my grandmother, who spent a lot of time with me when I was small. I thought about all the women on earth who gave birth to the child in human history. I deeply respect all the women who went through the process. The pain was in my imagination. Although I had a big fear before the birth of my daughter, after my daughter was born, my love for her just flooded like a fountain. I don't have any problem loving her. I am present 100% for her. I like being with her. It was a great and happy surprise.

My mother passed away last August. Six weeks after her death, I noticed that I was pregnant with my second child. I was very confused by the death and birth of lives. Since I have had difficulty understanding my sister for a long time, I am afraid that the child will be a girl. And it turned out to be a girl. I am now afraid that the relationship between my first and second children will not work well as the relationship between me and my sister. However, this time I want to believe that there is a possibility that it will work out. We can't live only on fear, right?

Regarding my mother, I can understand her struggles and inner conflicts that she had at my age. If we could meet each other as friends of the same generation, we could be good friends and share our thoughts. It is an interesting experience to be the daughter of my mother and the mother of my daughter at the same time. Now I see things from two different points of view. I can understand my mother better.

The theme of this essay was the transition from a woman to a mother. I had a chance to give birth to my child, but I don't think it is necessary to give birth to be a mother. I believe being pregnant or giving birth doesn't make a woman a mother. Women who can't give birth can also transform from a woman to a mother. Because it's not only a physical transition; it's an emotional transition.

IV.5   My Story—Nina

Nina is in her early 30's. She comes from northern Europe. I translated her words from German into English. She wrote her story three years after her third, and she believes, last child was born. At the time she wrote this piece, she just came back to her studying to grow in a career as a pedagogist.

I was 19 years old when I met my husband and best friend. After ten years of being together, when we decided to start a family and our eldest daughter promptly made her way into the world, we were overjoyed. The pregnancy progressed smoothly, and we welcomed the growing belly and all the changes it brought. As the daughter of a freelance midwife, pregnancy and childbirth had always been the most natural thing in the world to me. So, it was clear from the beginning that I wanted to give birth to my child at home. I had complete trust in a woman's body and the power of nature. It was all the more shocking when suddenly, things didn't go as planned. As I passed my due date, I realized that a home birth might not be a given. The pressure for the baby to arrive increased, and the obstetrician at the hospital imposed deadlines. Fortunately, my mother, a midwife, was there to support me and advocate for more time, avoiding the need for induction. On my 30th birthday, 15 days after the due date, labor finally began. My husband and mother were by my side, supporting me every step of the way. Initially, everything progressed naturally until, during the pushing stage, the baby's head couldn't progress further, and the fetal heart rate became irregular. Then, my mother and the attending obstetrician decided with us that they needed to use a vacuum. A few minutes and a few more pushes later, my daughter Sophie entered the world, and I finally got to hold her in my arms. The happiness I felt made me forget all the pain and hardship immediately. The fact that I could give birth in a familiar environment still fills me with joy today. It took me some time to adjust to the fact that I needed medical assistance during my first birth. In the second pregnancy, we also planned a home birth. I had a strong desire for a natural birth without medical interventions. I was thrilled when the birth of my second daughter Jaël went smoothly and quickly. My third daughter Noemi was also born at home. Her birth was very special to me because my husband and I knew that we didn't want any more children. The short duration of labor and the fact that my strength didn't fail me until the end filled me with happiness and pride. I am infinitely grateful that I was able to bring three healthy, wonderful daughters into the world. I love watching my daughters grow up and being able to accompany them in their development. I love being their mom. As the children become more independent, I have more time and space for myself again, which I greatly appreciate and which does me good. I am glad to have a very interesting and fulfilling profession and, in addition to the beautiful but demanding family life of five, to have other aspects of life. I enjoy being independent again, experiencing something alone with my husband, and being able to tackle my own projects again. And I enjoy it every time I come home and my three daughters tell me with glowing eyes what moves them and what they have experienced. I am excited to see where our journey as a family and my journey as a mother and woman will take us.

IV.6   Elliott Kronenfeld, Parenting

> *Elliott is a man in his mid-fifty. He wrote his account as he was facing the empty nest phase of his parenthood. Talking to him helped me realize how dynamic and mutable is the embodied intersubjective relationship we establish with our children. We face ongoing bodily and emotional changes at each phase of their development. Unfortunately, since this book is on early parenthood I did not have a chance to expand on the full arc of challenges and changes we encounter as parents.*

The act of raising a child is a dynamic process that results in the redefinition of the parent in innumerable ways. This is a deeply personal account that I write on

the cusp of major change for my children and myself. The journey to this junc-
ture was impacted by strife and joy, challenge and ease, sacrifice and awakenings
to multiple new identities.

For context, it is important to know that I became a parent because of years of
arduous effort and determination. No one just woke up pregnant one day. As a
gay man, the journey to parenthood was expensive, socially challenging, legally
perilous and often very lonely. I decided to become a parent at the start of the
"gayby boom", before it was common for openly gay men to have children. The
gay men I knew who had found their way to parenthood were mostly exclusively
because of prior heterosexual unions. My journey would be one as an openly
gay man.

I found my choices were not clear cut and each had risk. While attempting
international adoption, I was faced with great discrimination for being an unmar-
ried man and was told multiple times that no agency would work with me, and no
country would accept my dossier for adoption simply because I was an unmar-
ried man. I moved to surrogacy, and after two devastating failed attempts with
two different traditional surrogates, I was beginning to lose hope and a lot of my
money. It was at this time that an adoption agency contacted me back and told me
there was a slim chance that I could travel to Moldova—a small, impoverished
country in Eastern Europe nestled between Ukraine and Romania—and bring
back a child. I took the risk and told myself that I would never lie about my
identity, regardless of the outcome. Several months later I met my son Michael
(2.5 years old) in an archaic, rundown orphanage in Chisinau. In the Moldovan
court, the judge never specifically asked if I was gay but rather asked if I liked
women. I answered honestly, saying I did and that I had many meaningful relationships with women in my life. The adoption went through, and the journey
home with a child in trauma being cared for by a parent in shock was unnerving
for both of us, to say the least. It took several months before we both felt bonded,
safe and connected. This time began to shift the core of my identity in ways that
I could not articulate at the time.

Raising a child who came from such poverty, did not speak English, was
deeply malnourished, had never seen traffic or even wore a diaper before he met
me meant that we both were doing the work of bringing two disparate worlds
together. He eyed me with great suspicion but quickly learned I was the key
to food and getting to the park. I had to learn that all the skills and personal
power I believed I had, which were successful professionally, would have no
impact here. I needed a complete redefinition. Who I was as a person was quickly
shifted. My understanding of the world and how it operates was adjusted. My
world and his were not the same. The journey to merging them fundamentally
changed both of us.

This child who came from nothing fought for everything. Everything was
a battle. He was stubborn, fierce, outspoken and determined. I learned what

self-advocacy was from a toddler in a manner that no adult had ever shown me. As Michael began to trust me and let me into his world, I also learned the power that protection, intention, consistency, patience and healthy boundaries bring to the security of human connection. Who I was as a human was rapidly changing. Every interaction I had with the outside world was colored.

Two years after bringing Michael home, I decided to act on the deposits I had paid to the surrogacy agency and would try one more time—this time moving to gestational surrogacy. No longer would I be relying on intrauterine insemination and traditional surrogacy. [This is the process where the surrogate receives semen injected into her uterus in the hope that her ovulating will result in a positive pregnancy using her egg.] I wanted more security and guarantee, so I moved to gestational surrogacy, where I had a separate egg donor and gestational carrier, and we completed a full in vitro fertilization process. The surrogate would not be biologically connected to the child. After several months of waiting and discussing with various players in the process, I was connected with a terrific egg donor and then a special surrogate. The three of us worked well together with a clinic in Los Angeles (we all lived in different states), and the result was a positive pregnancy test. My daughter, Olivia, was born by cesarean delivery nine months later in Clovis, CA.

I had expected that I was an experienced parent having gone through so much with Michael, but I had never parented a newborn. A new set of skills was required, and I had to return to a place of not knowing and reduced confidence as I learned how to be present again.

Olivia has been easy, affable, peaceful, generous and kind from her first breath. She is in many ways the opposite of Michael. Where Michael's fierceness is grounded in personal expansion, Olivia's is centered on her environment and the relationships around her. Michael's love and kindness are protected with caution, but ever present, Olivia's is free flowing. Both are smart quick thinkers but take their space and use their powers differently. Seeing the uniqueness of each human in front of me taught me that parenting is not a global experience but one that is contextualized and nuanced with each child.

Parenting is a dynamic process. It is fluid and never static. Every moment is unique and changes you. I have come to realize that much like the times I would put an outfit on my child and see that it was too small and wonder how they grew so fast because it fit just last week, I am also growing and changing as quickly.

Parenting is not for the weak and lazy. Parenting is a master class for those who are willing to learn. The first realization is that parenting is about reparenting yourself. There is a fundamental shift in the scripts and stories that one grows up with and how they understand themselves. Once you become a parent, it is impossible not to reflect on the experiences you had with your parents— for better or worse—and try to make judgments about whether or not you will align with those experiences. You begin to rethink and reformulate your own childhood. You reposition yourself in your own memory as you make choices about how to move ahead with your child and must reconsider the conditions your own parents were in as they made choices that might have confused you. It is this remembering and recontextualizing that forces you to change your positionality on your whole being and history.

You also begin to realize that the job of parenting is not what you had been socialized to believe. Before meeting my children, I had a clear conception that I would raise these children to be strong and vibrant community members with high values and ethics. I would control their influence and TV watching, how they thought about the world, and how they would behave. I quickly learned that was not the job at all. It became clear early on that my children came fully formed and everything was pretty much already hardwired internally. Of course, I was mindful that I had to keep my children safe, teach them basic life skills and ensure they were fed and alive in their beds at night. It did not take long for me to understand that attending to the basics of parenting was the low hanging fruit. The true challenge in parenting is about unpacking and discovering who your child is and helping them to make sense of their world. This requires the ability to understand that my children will neither see the world the way I do nor will they share all my values. It was shocking how early I had to challenge my own perceived sense of power and control as my children grew into their unique, vibrant selves. Every lesson I learned with Michael was not applicable to the lessons I had to learn with Olivia. Each child emerged uniquely, and my *unpacking* and *interpreting* had to be relearned with each of them according to their internal gifts and challenges.

As each child progressed, I had to learn over and over again to go back to the start and relearn for that particular development stage. As a reasonably fully formed adult, the need to go back to the position of "I don't know" was deeply humbling. I had to accept my vulnerabilities openly. It challenged my own narratives of what it meant to be a man and a grownup. I had to acknowledge that I was giving power up to my children to drive their own existence according to their needs. This was nothing akin to anything I had been told about parenting prior to meeting my children.

This dynamic personal growth and adaptation do not slow down as the children become adults. I am in the early stages of empty nesting. Knowing that my children no longer share many aspects of their lives with me, or when they do, they are deeply edited. I am no longer capable of having the proximity of space to witness and watch daily. Accepting this reduction in experience does not mean that my children have a reduced value for me, but their needs are changing. I have spent more than 20 years actively parenting daily, and now I may not talk to them every day. As they enter into adult relationships and think about forming lasting adult relationships, my role shifts again. I have gone from family to family of origin/extended family. Their partners and children—if they have them—are their newly created core family. To be able to hold the emotional security that moving to this new positionality does not indicate a reduction of importance or connection, but a shift in role and purpose. To be successful in this new role, I must honor their agency and independence or risk creating a fissure because I have not evolved along with them.

I have instilled in my children that family is defined as those that give identity and security and who you give the same in return. Others that are bound to you by blood or legal status are relatives. This definition has given me comfort that there is still a role in sharing identity and security, but I am no longer the primary person to do that.

The continued human development that is my life now means that I must go back to the skills I learned in parenting my children. The self-reparenting experience starts again. I must unpack who I am now and who I am evolving to be. There is a constant challenge of what being the parent of adult children is going to be as compared to an adult that is making choices with myself as the primary stakeholder. There is a persistent exploration of who I want to be as a fully formed being that is not spending most of my time and resources on dependents. My sense of connectedness to my adults [I don't call them my kids anymore] looks and feels different, and that can be challenging for me—and that is my work to do now.

IV.7 *Becoming Something Like a Mother, Maren Wehrle*

> *Maren is an established scholar, a phenomenologist like me. Originally from Germany she is raising her daughter in the Netherlands. We both became pregnant at the same time. Even though I never had the pleasure to meet her in person, during the pregnancy and afterwards we had the chance to exchange our impressions about this journey. I felt very close to her. She gave me the courage to share more of myself in this book about this incredible experience.*

Actually, I never wanted to marry and have kids, out of principle. At least I was consequent with regard to the first principle. Growing up in a little town with an almost absent dad, who as a driver saw more of the roads of the world (or at least in eastern and western Europe) than of me growing up, and a stay-at-home (single) mum. Since, I can think, I dreamt of going away. In my coming-of-age years, I identified with Hermann Hesse's cliché novel The Steppenwolf (which was actually about men in their last quarter of life), The Catcher in the Rye or Kerouac's On the Road, or films like Train Spotting or Pulp Fiction. All in which women played mostly sexy sidekick roles. Not that I was aware of or bothered by this at the time; I just found myself always identifying with the other side, the lone wolf, about to discover the world, independent from anyone. My favorite song was "I am a rolling stone" by Bob Dylan or Boys Don't Cry by the Cure.

Quite funny for someone who got stuck in the Black Forest until she was 20 and then only made it to the nearby Freiburg to study philosophy (to annoy her dad mostly), because anything further away just was way out of her league, confidence or economic possibilities.

Twenty-four years later, I am finding myself being a mother of a nearly two-year-old child. How did that happen? My principle lasted quite a while; I only came to change my mind about it when I turned 40. I never felt an explicit desire to get children or had the feeling of missing out. However, I came across a partner who I could imagine quite well as a father. Someone who did not necessarily need starting a family to feel complete but had the courage and curiosity to be open for it. One day he just said very calmly but was convinced, "[M]aybe we should at least try or leave the option open, otherwise we might regret it someday". I went quiet and felt a little panic, but then said okay.

It turned out that principle (or the fact that I was engaged in the rat race to survive and get a paid job as a philosopher) was not the only reason; I was hesitant of starting a family. Most of all, I was anxious of being trapped by being a mum, of gender expectations, loss of freedom and independence, ending up as my mother, someone with big dreams and capacities, betrayed by her social class and history, stuck in the immanence (as Simone de Beauvoir would call it) of a town in the Black Forest, waiting for her husband to come home. But I was also more directly and physically scared: the fear of being pregnant and giving birth, the changes my body will undergo, the development of another body in me, the responsibility that comes with it, the pain and total loss of control.

If I had had the choice, I would have loved being a father instead; this seemed a lot more fun. Being a father, in my experience (and this is still the case for most of my academic and non-academic friends and people I know), means that you gain something additionally to your life; you can continue work and live (mostly) as before, only that you now also have kids. Kids you can do something fun with, who await you when you come home, who adore and love you, because the time you spend with them is precious. Of course, this picture is way more complicated with the responsibility and the bad consciousness that comes with the traditional gender role model for man, and which is also a heavy burden to take. I am very much aware of this, but for the sake of this first-person perspective, I allow myself to oversimplify and represent a sharpened and sarcastic view. Take, for example, the expression "working mum"; "working" is in this context a special adverb to be added to one's ontological entity, a (often problematized or emphasized) surplus. No one would even think about speaking of a "working dad", as this is the most self-evident it can get.

Being a mum, or so I feared, means that your whole life changes; nothing stays the same, neither you, nor your body, nor your work, nor your identity. And it turned out that I was quite right.

When we decided to let the option open, it was clear from the start that I intended to work full-time again after the 16 weeks of maternal leave. In the Netherlands, where I live and work, this is luckily normal. In Germany, however, where I come from, you are strongly morally obliged and economically motivated to stay at home at least for one full year (of course only as a mother) and then forced to work part-time (if at all) because no proper daycare infrastructure is provided, or it doesn't pay off due to specific tax regulations, that benefits a one provider model.

For my partner and me, it went without saying that we wanted to share the responsibility, care and economic burdens equally or better, according to our individual work and life situations. This was easy to decide, as we both earn almost equally (also an advantage of being an old mother or choosing for a partner your age or younger). Regarding my work as a tenured professor, being able to travel and stay overnight from the beginning was important to me. For my job, I commute from Amsterdam to Rotterdam, and I am invited for talks or conferences on a regular basis. So, it was clear that we should take over all caring tasks equally from the beginning to make this work.

This is what we discussed and agreed on before, and I must say, it all worked out well; no problems on this front. We were very lucky to have a daycare facility (open 12 hours a day) within five minutes walking distance and a grandma, happy to care for little Emma one day a week or in emergencies or to allow us to go out for a night. Most families are not as privileged as us, so I am very thankful for this. Despite all privileges, social and economic circumstances (my tenure got through during my paternal leave time), an engaged and truly emancipated and loving father, and a healthy, happy and easy child, I must say: being a parent or more specifically a mum (from my perspective) really has changed my life, and identity, and no, despite all thinking or maybe because of it, I was definitely not prepared for this.

My pregnancy was, despite my anxieties and concerns beforehand, and despite my age and the fact that I had to inject myself blood thinners every day because of a medical history, an interesting and mostly pleasant experience. I never felt so optimistic, relaxed, happy, fit and confident, all because of the hormones; it's magical. Ok, the last weeks before birth were tough, with more than 30 degrees every day, nothing to do but wait or prepare for birth, an event, and a pain you cannot even imagine, despite all preparation courses and literature. In these last weeks, you cannot properly sleep or eat anymore, as the belly is unproportional and heavy, and the little one inside lies where your organs once were and reminds you (luckily) of its existence by kicking regularly.

The body or legs of your little one, if it is already in a birthing position, literally lie heavy on your chest, causing permanent acid reflux, stomach pain and problems breathing. So, yes, you are really waiting for the birth to happen in the end, despite your fear. And yes, you finally want to see and meet the little human that was growing all the time inside you, that you feel is so close and part of you but at the same time so far away and alien.

From the beginning, with all the echo's and checks you do, you come to see this being growing, from a little bean to a human-like-looking creature. You caress your belly; you speak with it; at least I did constantly, more to reassure or calm myself than to actually interact, but anyway. It was strange to feel something living and moving in your body; at the same time, I never felt alone; I carried something/someone with me; she was always with me, which gave me a warm and confident feeling. This also made me behave and take responsibility differently; everything I did was also to support her well-being and protect her. I can imagine that this gives people a (deeper) meaning in life if they did not have one before.

We early on did give our little bean a name, when the biological sex could be identified, Emma. I thought, even when something will happen, she at least has a name. And it felt strange to me to address her with a neutral pronoun or non-binary name, despite my feminist and queer convictions. Although I did not want to address her in gendered ways too early, and as a person, I really hate all this gender reveal stuff and the binary between light blue and rose that terrorizes you from the beginning. As if all of this would or should matter (apart from economic reasons, of course, as you can sell every stuff twice, one time in light blue and the other in rose). However, I needed to give the little bean a name, and I must admit that I was really happy when it came out that she would be a girl and already expected it that way (and so did my partner). It seems that despite critical and rational convictions, deep-felt habits, cliché desires or what is familiar to you, sometimes you gain the upper hand within these limit existential situations.

As little Emma wanted to stay a little longer as a subtenant in my body, but regarding my age (42 at that time), I did not want to take any risks, so we decided to induce birth after I was one week overdue. On paper, I had an ideal "natural" (except the induction, of course) and gave birth to a healthy child after 12 hours, no complications, not even stitches needed. I entered the hospital at 7 a.m. and left the same day shortly before midnight with my partner and baby (also because they needed the bed, of course, and I was able to somehow move). Still, this was a limit experience, with immense pain and feelings of anxiety and complete helplessness. For most women, birth is traumatic, not only due to complications and pain but also due to the circumstances, that is, how you are treated in hospital.

First of all, the whole thing is not about you, your pain, body or state of mind is not as important; your body is in the service of giving birth, the main medical goal is to guarantee the survival and successful birth of the child (which includes your well-being to a certain extent, of course).

Things are being done with you, and decisions over your body are being made, at times without being communicated or explained to you. In the best case, this is because it is urgent and you yourself cannot speak or communicate properly anymore (because of the pain); in the worst case, you feel like a statistic in your own birth, observing it as if from a distance, and suffering on your own (but probably not in silence). There is nothing scarier if nurses or doctors suddenly act as if in panic and you neither know what happens nor can do anything yourself.

But back to my case, I entered the hospital at 7 am; due to a lack of personal, I had to wait until 10 am, then they first picked open the fruit sac, which did not cause pain but felt extremely weird, uncomfortable, embarrassing and being at the mercy of others as you lie there nearly naked, dripping all the time. Then they started to induce birth with a hormone infusion that should open your birth canal (canal must be 10 cm open for the real birth/press contractions to start). You need to breathe in a specific way to help this process; after four hours, I thought I was proudly and already quite tired to have done almost half the work, but in fact nearly nothing had happened (not 1 cm), so they turned up the hormone volume. Within one to two hours, the canal opened from 1 to 10 cm; it went so quick and was so painful that I felt totally exhausted and was barely able to speak, so I gave my partner the signal, that I cannot take it anymore and asked for medication/painkillers. Unfortunately, this was too late. Within this whole process, six hours, I was alone (except my partner) and different nurses and doctors came in from time to time to check on me.

I cannot even remember any face or name. No one told me what to do or if what I was doing was right (is there a right/wrong here?). After having been told that pain medication was no option anymore and that they would start with the actual birth/pressing phase, I still had to wait in pain for nearly two hours until one doctor and nurse were available. I really do not know how I managed this. By this time, the real contraction had started. This really feels as if a demon possessed your body; you see yourself act and scream in ways you never would have imagined. For others, this must look like an exorcism; maybe that is where all the horror stories and films got their inspiration from. Behaving like this, totally out of control, producing strange and never-heard noises, feels really alienating, but at this point in the procedure, you do not care anymore, as the pain has taken over your body completely.

Moreover, because of the artificial hormone doses, I got uncontrollable body shakings. I can still remember how I tried clinging my arms and legs to the hospital bed in the most unnatural ways, while some other doctor who came to check on me tried to calm me down so that I would not hurt myself. Then finally, one doctor and one nurse came and stayed to get this through with me to the end. What a relief, finally someone to give you instructions, motivate and support you, telling you what happens next and that you are nearly there (haha, this is of course a lie, at least in the first hour(s), but helps nonetheless). They call it labor, and rightly so, I successfully finished two marathons, in New York and Berlin, and they were nothing compared to this, not in terms of physical effort, exhaustion or pain.

Still, it is a special or productive pain, as it is necessary to give birth and thus helps you in achieving your goal. And when you are assured that the little one inside is doing all right during the whole process, you feel related to it in body and faith. You are not alone in doing this, not the only one for whom this is a real existential struggle and wonder.

I had my eyes closed during the whole process to better concentrate, focus on the contractions and bear the pain, and also because I did not want to see anything of me or them. Your partner, who really wants to help and support you, cannot do a thing except wiping away the sweat and tears from your face, and it must be really difficult to see your partner suffering and fighting like this without being able to do anything, just being helpless.

When they said it was time to open my eyes, I was almost not quick enough; after all these hours, it still came unexpectedly. I heard the crying and opened my eyes, and the whole tiny body of little Emma was 2 cm before my eyes. Yes, indeed, what a moment when the baby is finally lying on your chest, searching instinctively for your breast and starts suckling. It is not describable or even imaginable that this little human creature really lived all this time inside your body. It is an immense relief, warmth and love that fills your body; pain is gone immediately (at least for now), and you fall immediately in love with this little creature, no matter how it looks after hours of struggle; for you, it is just perfect. In the best and worst possible way, you recognize that we, or better yet, you yourself, are nothing but a mammal (I never thought I would quote this awful song by ever by the bloodhound gang; please forgive me).

The next weeks and months (I stayed at home with pregnancy leave and vacation for four months) are an emotional rollercoaster of happiness, anxiety, panic, crying and happiness. Your old life and all its self-evidence have gone. You find yourself in a strange monotonous and repetitive circle determined by the most existential needs of a baby: food/feeding (every two hours), sleep (every two hours) and digestion (every three hours). You live in a closed spatial and temporal bubble, tethered to your bed or home (as you are not able to properly move or sit) and lose every sense of time and reality.

At the same time, especially when you are breastfeeding, you are all body; you, your needs or person are not important anymore. You also feel extremely insecure as you do not know (yet) what the baby needs or wants or what to do. You feel guilty and a real loser if the breastfeeding doesn't work out or you do not get your baby or your body in the right drinking positions (it takes, in general, more than a week before this technically and bodily works out, and most women give up in despair when they do not receive proper supervision by nurses or midwives). Bodily, breastfeeding is a very intense experience, in the positive and the negative. Before the milk is ready, it mostly hurts; you have inflammations; your breasts get hard as stone; you get a fever; while breastfeeding, it mostly hurts (for many women) in the beginning; nipples are sore and need to be treated etc. Also, it feels like your breasts are no longer part of you but of a strange new body in service of feeding your child. They change in form and quantity to such an extent that you do not even feel ashamed if someone would see them in public (while breastfeeding) because they do in no way remind you of your former old bodily self.

To make a long story short, although it can be an extreme intimate, warm, powerful (you are the only one who can feed and calm down your child!) and even sensory/erotic feeling. Most of the time, especially in the beginning, it feels technical, mechanic, alienating and artificial, thus far from self-evident and natural. And as said, you will never feel more like a mammal, reduced to your body and feeding capacities. It is not as if you build up a personal bond with your child; it is a purely bodily relationship, all smell and touch.

For me, the first four months were the toughest. After the first two weeks, where you are full of hormones and enjoy the extraordinary situation, being supported by your partner (who has two weeks of birth leave) and the midwife care service, who help you with everything, be it related to baby care, household chores or preparing food for you. People come visit you, you get loads of presents and the little one mostly sleeps in these first two weeks. But afterwards, the real challenge begins.

Suddenly you are being alone at home with a baby you hardly know, on service 24 hours a day, anxious and insecure most of the time, unable to take a break or sleep properly. Of course, there is this immense love for the little one that fills you, but mostly this love was experienced by me as concern. Every time she cried, my whole body was shaking; I was alert (will she cry or not) all the time. Six weeks after birth, I went with little Emma for the first time for a walk in the stroller to my last appointment with the midwife. I was so tensed, alert and anxious that she would begin to cry again (what they do when they are not used to riding around with a stroller) that I lost my way, came late, was covered in sweat and felt exhausted. In retrospect, I cannot imagine why this was so difficult or why I was so anxious or tensed. As you get used to the crying and are able to anticipate the behavior of your little one, you know when it is serious and when it is just a crying hour. This continuous tension and alertness were unbearable; I felt as if I was going to get crazy or psychotic.

It went worse when Emma was seriously sick for the first time. One night, when she was coughing a lot and stopped breathing for a moment, Michel and I immediately had the feeling, okay, this is serious. But I was so anxious and in panic that I couldn't react properly; my whole body was shaking. Luckily, he did the right thing, calling the weekend ambulance, organizing a drive (we do not have a car) and getting her to the doctor. In the end, everything turned out fine, but I couldn't sleep for the next two weeks. Every time she coughed or showed any sign of sickness, I started shivering and panicking again. This only ended after she turned five months, and I stopped breastfeeding, and the hormones went back to normal.

The first day we brought Emma to daycare after four months, although difficult at first because I felt kind of guilty, was such a relief. I came home and the first thing I did was sleep for two hours. Being back at work slowly gave me back my old confidence and identity, and I turned into a much more relaxed and sovereign mother, at last. Now, I was looking forward to spending time with my baby, no longer overwhelmed and chained to my home. Also, little Emma developed a much steadier rhythm, slept better and cried less after she went to daycare from Monday to Wednesday, and on Thursdays she spent the day with her grandma. On Fridays, my partner took care of her, as he took parental leave in the first year (and I in the second year).

So being back at work was really a kind of vacation in the beginning compared to full-time motherhood, although my academic job is far from a normal nine-to-five job.

However, working full-time again as an academic came with other challenges. Academic life, its routines and expectations are not made for mums or engaged parents. Even though, in principle, I can work eight to nine hours a day (with provided day care) for five days a week, it still is a planning struggle. For the first time, the implicit rule of academic life became obvious and a real problem. To get everything done, from teaching, academic supervision, organization and management, and still have some time to do research, 40 hours a week are not enough.

Before, I usually worked late hours, on weekends, and took holidays to work on articles or book projects. This is not possible anymore; every evening colloquium with drinks, every late meeting, conference, workshop or talk abroad must be planned months ahead and negotiated with the working agenda of your partner. Going for a conference (mostly on Fridays and Saturdays) means that your partner either has to take vacation (to accompany you) or has to stay the whole weekend at home with your child and has no time left for whatsoever (as baby's up to two or three years do not occupy themselves, but want to be entertained and accompany you even when you have to visit the bathroom). Getting this time from your partner means thus that they will miss time for themselves and that you will in turn get less leisure time, that is, time to spend for yourself or with friends. To make a long story short. Even in the most ideal circumstances, you end up with nearly no time for either research or yourself, while continuously hearing from (mostly) male colleagues: ah, we don't see you around anymore so often. It is probably because you are "mothering" now, want to be with your child all the time, and philosophy and meeting colleagues are less important to you.

No, I am not so much around because I have to use all the time I get as effectively as possible and thus have no time for chitchat, drinking coffee or lunch with colleagues or even going for drinks after a seminar, not because I do not want to or would enjoy it, but simply because otherwise everything would fall apart—my work, my daily arrangements and my relationship. And here, I haven't even mentioned sleep deprivation and being sick all the time (because the little one builds up an immunity system with the help of all kinds of viruses that he kindly gets from other kids in daycare), which is an essential part of early parenthood. To end the work part on a positive note, I really enjoy going to conferences and when I have a day where I am able to work on an article, reading and writing on my desk. Compared to a "working day" with a little one, this is, believe me— even compared to the most stressful deadline days in academics—pure vacation. The peace and quiet, the privilege to read, think and be able to write about topics one is interested in, or listening to talks by others, discussing, eating and drinking with (hopefully) inspiring colleagues, getting questions and feedback, appreciation or critique for your talk, to whom (most) of the people actually listen; and last but not least, the privilege to properly sleep (until 8 am!) and having everything organized and meals prepared for you. How wonderful is this!

However, it is also different in another way. While I am writing this early in the morning, I am about to head off to the workshop I am presenting in Montreal, Canada, an eight-hour flight away from home. And although I enjoy this stay, the academic exchange and the time for myself immensely, I find myself missing little Emma. This was less the case when she was still a baby (before she turned one year and older). Now that she really is a little person with a will, humor and her own little way of speaking, dancing and laughing, and because of the personal relation and bond we have built up within the last 20 months, I start missing her more every time. I miss how she immediately shouts "eeeeten" (eeeeeating/foooood) with a huge smile on her face, much to the sound of a football supporter, every time we enter a restaurant or café or when I let her know that dinner is ready. I miss how she raises both arms in the air rhythmically to express her joy when she hears there is a "toetje" (dessert) or we will eat pasta ("paaaaaastaaaaa!"). I miss how she brings me her shoes and jacket and demands me to go outside with her to play ball "mama buiten (outside)", even if it is just 6 a.m. in the morning. I miss how she immediately starts moving her body and dances whenever we turn on the music. I also miss when she throws herself on the ground whenever she is frustrated that she does not get what she wants, or when the objects and world show their resistance to her will. I miss how she touches me suddenly in my face, eyes, nose and ears and speaks the names of these body parts out loud, proud that she could identify them, and also as if she wants to reassure herself that they are still there. I miss the joy and fascination in her eyes and whole body when she sees a little ant, points to it as "Ameis" (luckily here she uses a variation of the German word "Ameise") and observes it with respect and wonder. I miss how she takes my hand before she falls asleep in her own little bed. I have the routine to sit there like this for at least five minutes, with her hand in mine, while she breathes slowly and peacefully.

This is to make sure that she is asleep (this is so relieving, especially when it took quite a while before she actually fell asleep), and it is also so much more.

The most peaceful and quiet moment at the end of the day, me sitting next to her bed, looking at this creature, lying like all babies do, on their knees with their little bum in the air, and at least within these five minutes a big warm wave is filling my whole body and the feeling that everything is going to be alright.

In the last 21 months, it is as if not only she developed into a little person but also I have finally become something as a mother, for the best and for the worst of it.

IV.8   When I Did (Not) Become a Mother, Emanuela De Bellis[3]

> *Emanuela is a psychologist and a musician in her early forties. To me, she is an ever-present friend, making it difficult to write anything that feels academic or somewhat detached about her. Observing her experience has helped me realize that motherhood does not begin and end with the birth of a child.*

> Tenderness has its own fragile inner time, that of a present not closed in on itself, but open to the past, to memory, and to the future, to waiting and hope. A time that is that of waiting and lingering, of silence and attention.
>
> —E. Borgna

Demetra: Overflowing With Emotion

The first notable experience was with Demetra, a child who signified a profound shift in my life. Although Kalou might have initiated this change subtly and gradually, it was with Demetra that I felt an irreversible transformation.

Demetra, at 7 years old, was born prematurely and had several challenges, including psychomotor delays and impending blindness due to retinopathy of prematurity (ROP). She was a delicate child who loved music and was part of our music workshops for young children. Although she wasn't my direct student, I was involved in her progress as a school psychologist. My role was to support students with various difficulties, ensuring they were on the right musical path, monitoring their progress and providing support to both teachers and parents—a role centered around care.

The Christmas recital is always the most magical event for me, perhaps due to its symbolism of light and its appeal to children, mixing anticipation and wonder. This year, the anticipation was even more personal, as I had recently discovered I was pregnant. I was filled with my own blend of anticipation and wonder.

While guiding the children backstage, preparing for the recital, I noticed Demetra was unusually quiet amidst the excitement. Suddenly, she called out for her mother, a sign that she was overwhelmed by the emotions. My usual professional strategies seemed inadequate at that moment. Instead, a profound tenderness emerged within me, transforming my approach. Holding her hand, I reassured her, "Don't be afraid, I'm here with you". She clung to my hand, and we joined the others.

Little did I know, shortly after the recital, that I would learn that I was losing my baby. This experience introduced a tenderness that never left me, deeply influencing my interactions with children. It shifted my approach from merely assisting to actively nurturing, transcending the professional to a deeply personal level. Borgna describes tenderness as a bridge that allows us to step outside ourselves and connect with others' inner worlds. This bridge, once built, remains steadfast despite the pain and losses I later faced.

Kalou: Learning Boundaries

Kalou, an Eritrean child adopted by an Anglo-Italian couple, joined our school just a month before the Christmas recital. She was pure joy and vitality, eager to communicate despite the language barrier, and full of enthusiasm. Shortly after meeting her, I dreamt of being told I was pregnant after mistakenly thinking I was terminally ill, a dream that left me feeling unexpectedly positive and peaceful. This dream was prophetic; a pregnancy test confirmed I was indeed pregnant for the first time.

Kalou's exuberance felt like an announcement of my own impending motherhood. However, I realized the importance of maintaining boundaries. Kalou was not only a symbol of my joy but also an individual with her own needs and energy. My role was to guide her energy into the world, not to impose my emotions on her. This realization helped me channel my joy into a more attentive, yet relational, stance.

This understanding deepened after my miscarriage. Despite my grief, I continued to interact with Kalou, learning to balance my emotions without overwhelming her. This balance became a lesson in parenthood—caring deeply without overstepping the boundaries of the child's space.

Reflecting on my unborn children, I view them with the same tenderness I extend to the children I work with. This tenderness overflows from within, encompassing both joy and sorrow and continues to shape my approach to nurturing and caregiving.

This deeply human, almost transcendental experience of tenderness transforms our interactions, allowing us to care genuinely and connect profoundly with others. As Borgna suggests, this tenderness bridges the gap between our subjectivity and the inner worlds of those we care for, creating a lasting impact on both sides.

IV.9   You, Me and the Mother, Susi Ferrarello

I became a mother when I lost Martino. That's the name I chose for the cluster of cells that were forming in my womb a few weeks after the stick turned positive. I've always wanted to become a mother, but for different reasons something wasn't right. I did not want to become a mother like my mother (although I loved her dearly) and create a family like hers. I need to grow up a bit as a person before starting my own family. Only then could I have found the right partner and had a chance to become the right mother. This growth took long years to unfold. I'm 38 and having a cocktail in Basel with my now husband when I told him that I'm finally ready to try. A few weeks later, I start feeling very tired, suddenly super hungry and then very emotional. I took a pregnancy test, and to our immense joy, it turned out to be positive. I was going to become a mother. Yet, things didn't go well from the start. Maybe the same day I took the test I started cramping. I did not know what that meant. It was Mother's Day. I was having tea in a café near Basel with my partner when they brought me a complimentary cookie. The package outside read—'i biscotti di nonna Annunziata'. I could not believe it. That is not such a common name; my mother's name was Annunziata. She passed away eight years before then. It felt like a hug at such a special moment. I wished her a happy Mother's Day, thinking that soon I would have been a mother too.

As I said, things started going bad pretty soon. I was in a country I knew very little about. I depended on my partner for almost anything. He was giving his 100% at work, also in preparation for the new role he was taking as a father. It was hard to wait for his return from work as I started bleeding. We went to the ER. Another young couple was there. She was crying a lot. I was much older than she. We were so different but so close to each other nonetheless. It's my turn. Doctors say that it's hard to tell, but most probably everything is going well. After that visit, the world seemed to come back to color again. We enjoyed a small walk along the Rein and let ourselves go wild on some dreams, knowing that still ten days were ahead of us before our three months' check. Life passed not only with its usual duties but also with more doubts, questions and dreams. I chose a name for that life. I knew it was too early, but that name came into my head, and I couldn't let it go. I felt so ambivalent though. I desired to have this baby, but my working situation was still so unstable, and I lived in such a foreign country with such a difficult language. Would I still have been able to become myself as this baby came to this world?

As I battled against these questions, it became more and more evident to me that something was going wrong. I arrived at the gynecologist very weak and almost incapable of standing. We waited almost an hour before she could visit us for the appointment. As she pointed the cursor of the ultrasound at my belly, I still hoped for a miracle. I knew that my optimistic husband was almost certain to hear a heartbeat that day. But nothing showed up. The cells stopped multiplying along with our dreams. The doctor caught my husband's disappointment and said in Swiss German without my understanding—didn't you know that one out of three women experience this? What did you expect?

She gave me the card of a psychologist to talk to. As I left the office, I melted into tears without knowing well what was expected of me. In the following days, I remember the sense of hopelessness, fear and vulnerability I experienced. The doctor asked me to wait for the body to spontaneously expel "the material" (that material already had a name for me, so much I had desired to get pregnant before). After ten obnoxious days in which I had to learn how to walk around the world with this now-dead life inside of me, which just a few days before was the promise of new dreams and projects, she gave me pills that would have facilitated its expulsion. The language gap made everything more uncertain; she was speaking German while my first language was Italian. I was not sure I understood all that there was to do. I remember I came back home taking these pills and started cramping alone on my couch. After a few hours of contractions—to my expense, I discovered that not only birthing women experience contractions but miscarrying ones, too—the blood starts coming. Plenty of blood. In my ingenuity, I had bought for myself a package of chips and another package of chocolate chip cookies, thinking that that was all I needed. Little did I know that the affair of miscarrying a fetus was a much more serious deal. Nobody prepared me for what I faced. I was carrying myself from the couch to the bathroom. Flushing the toilet with bloody material of the baby I desired to have for all my life; it was psychologically devastating, but even more was the pain. In the end, my sister's call saved me. She was in Italy; I was in Switzerland. By that time, I had lost quite an amount of blood. She asked me how many pills I had already taken. I told her that I was not sure if I should keep taking those pills at the same rate as my doctor suggested. She encouraged me to call the doctor again to check. It was impossible to get her on the phone. Eventually I ended up calling an emergency doctor. Everyone was talking in German, which I barely understood. Finally, a woman understood that I was Italian and started speaking in that language. She guided me step by step about what to do. After a few hours, the blood quieted down, and so did the cramps. I managed to fall asleep. For all that time, it did not cross my mind for even one second to call for help. My sister called just out of personal care. In the evening, my husband arrived and saw me just a little more tired than usual. That blood was mine. That moment of desperation and pain was supposed to be all mine. That day I became a mother, even though it was just blood and empty dreams. Probably I wanted to be alone. I did not know how to let anyone else enter that complicated psychological and physical space. Before that, I thought of miscarriages as little moments of illness comparable to a fever or the flu. My mother had some, but I never fully understood.

It took a long time to recover. In one of my walks through the forest, I found a little pebble as small as he was when his cells left my body, and I wrote his name and date on it. I'm still very jealous of that little pebble on my desk. Although I wanted to try to have another baby soon after, my husband said that there was not enough love to welcome another life in our home. Very sadly, I thought he was right. For my part, I was very much in rage toward myself (wasn't I ambiguous about his arrival?) and toward him (where was he when I was in pain?). My job was still very insecure, and now the pandemic was adding a halo of uncertainty to all our lives.

A few months before the pandemic obliged all of us to stop, the job took a better shift, but it required me to move back to the States alone. I spent the pandemic years mending my wounds, reflecting on what happened and finally accepting death. I think it was only when I arrived at accepting that the worst could have happened to me in pregnancy, delivery or motherhood that things started taking a new direction. Within a few months, I got married with my partner, and we got pregnant. I did my first trimester alone (another very good time to meditate), and then he reached me in California, where he found a good job. I enjoyed my pregnancy to the fullest. The first trimester I bled at any time I was moving or taking a walk. That was a trigger for me. But then, as my husband came, the last two semesters were lovely. I cooked and ate lots of good food. I spent time on the phone with my sister and friends and took long walks on the beach. I considered the option of paying a doula to help us since we were alone in the United States to face such a change, but I didn't really click with anyone, and I preferred to spend that money on a family trip we could have taken later.

In 2022, on the second of the three days of labor to deliver my baby, a nurse came to my bed to convince me to insert a tube to check on the vitals of my baby. I could not move. I was attached to monitors and IVs to receive antibiotics. I was having an at-risk pregnancy because of my age (42) and the time of labor was adding to it, so I asked the nurse if it was strictly necessary to insert this tube. After all, I was already connected to fetal monitoring during the whole labor to check on my baby's vitals. She said that it was not necessary, but she was visibly concerned. Then the morning comes. I realize it only because a new shift starts and a new nurse comes. I was exhausted. My husband was asleep. The new nurse doesn't ask. She checks something on the monitor, and she puts a tube inside me to further monitor my baby. Finally, after 72 hours of labor, I am ready to push. My baby comes out, and his head is bleeding. My husband and I are worried, although overwhelmed by the joy of seeing him for the first time. My husband asks what that bleeding was. The nurses mutter some excuses. Two days afterwards, I was discharged without any official explanation. What they told me was that my ribs hurt my baby while in the womb, hence the bleeding. Of course, an external pediatrician at the first visit confirmed that the scar (which will remain for all his life and fortunately will not bring him any particular neurological harm as far as we know) was due to the tube they inserted.

His arrival brought immense joy into my life. Love. Love. Love. That was the most I was feeling and receiving in return. I thought that if I had died without having children, I would have never experienced such a pure form of love. That made me feel a little compassion for the baby I was—a feeling that I keep experiencing as I am making parenting choices with my son. Every one of us deserves to experience such love in some way or another.

I thought that I wasted too much time on the wrong partners. I would have loved to have at least four of those little babies. I understood that after all, I was just trying to mother all of my partners, and reasonably, things could not work out. Moreover, I was still a very immature mother. Still today, I do not know what kind of mother I am. What I understood is that motherhood (maybe parenthood more at large) breaks you. If it's not because of the health, it is because of the sleeplessness or the marital problems it might bring with it. Motherhood breaks you so that you can put yourself together in a more loving (hopefully) better way. I had to grow up quite a bit since I became a mother. I had to learn more and more how to love myself, my family and my friends. Taking care of your spiritual growth while you do not even have time to pee is quite hard. I think that I became a worse person in the first months. I was overwhelmed with anxiety. I didn't give a break to myself or to my husband. It was just the two of us, and we needed to be a functional team. My child was and still is a very bad sleeper; his naps had been in my arms for at least the first ten months. I didn't have any help or any time for anything else. I was floating with him in this timeless bubble. When he was almost two months old, I suffered from a very bad mastitis that became a dangerous infection—despite that I never stopped breastfeeding sometimes while I was in tears of pain or even worse while I was devoured by sadness at the thought of having to stop providing him with my milk. Then I suffered from a virus for months. I lost more than 10 kilos in less than four months. I was exhausted. It was also incredibly difficult to provide for my care while being with him. Even phone calls to make doctor's appointments, finding the medicines and taking antibiotics were so difficult and stressful.

My husband used to take care of him from six to seven in the morning so that I could go to do some yoga. Doing exercises helped me to break with the sense of fragility and vulnerability I felt toward my body after pregnancy. I was growing stronger despite the exhaustion. I remember it felt (and still does) weird at times to walk on the street without him in my belly or in my arms. I was a new body, and it felt somewhat wrong that this didn't show in the world. At yoga while chit-chatting with others, a woman gave me a bad look and alarmingly said—are you really leaving your two-month-old baby alone at home with your husband? I was puzzled, and I felt slightly guilty. It's my husband, not a stranger, I thought. But still, it made me feel awkward. Or on the street, I was walking with my newborn in the stroller and talking over the phone with my friend. My baby started crying. So I walked back toward home to feed him. A few meters from home, a woman who seemingly walked beside me along the way while he was crying, stopped me and reproached me. To my understanding, she was trying to meet other people's eyes for approval and (consequent) public shaming. I couldn't let this poor baby cry—she said. Politely, I told her that if she let me, we would have soon been home ready for his nursing. Living as an immigrant or, in better terms, as an expat added to my anxiety because I couldn't completely understand how this country worked. Would they have randomly taken my baby from me?

Another cultural pressure that might have influenced me during this time was the work ethic. I never stopped working. Partly I chose so because I needed to come back to myself every now and then. I thought that my beloved job would have kept me anchored to something (I was wrong. There's no anchor in this massive revolution!). When I was still in the birthing room and they were cleaning me and my baby, I replied to a working email. That was crazy. I would never do that again, but I think the United States puts lots of pressure on working people. While he was just a few months old, I was promoted to tenured professor, plus I won an award for my research activities. In both cases, I couldn't attend the ceremony because I didn't have help with the baby. It's a pity that none from campus offered some helpful arrangement when I told them. On the other hand, I had very good luck with my department. My chair and colleagues were the sweetest people I could find. I attended most of my first faculty meetings with him in my arms while breastfeeding, and in longer meetings they encouraged me to bring him and took turns taking care of him.

When he was around ten months, he started suffering from breath-holding spells, meaning he would faint from lack of oxygen and turn blue when holding his breath while crying. I was boiling in anxiety. Now he is 19 months old; the breath spells are gone. It's been two months since he started going to a daycare three times a week with people that seem to care about his well-being. This gives me the serenity I need, to be (hopefully) myself in the world, to serve the world with what is needed. In doing so, I am coming back to be who I was and a new person I am trying to know every day a little bit better.

Notes

1 The full poem is entitled The Face of Old Women, and it is a poem about native women of the Vancouver Islands.
2 Since I am connected to these people and I want to respect their right to anonymity, I would give an account of their life but remain as general as possible about their personal information. I also edited the least possible of their first-hand accounts, as I found some of their typos an interesting lapsus of tongue.
3 Unfortunately, I received her text when the book was already closed and I could not be in dialogue with her lived experience.

Bibliography

Bergum, V. (1986). *The phenomenology of woman to mother* [Doctoral dissertation, University of Alberta; unpublished]. Retrieved from https://era.library.ualberta.ca/items/5bd71ea9-8026-4712-8865-ed8d6da810c2

Cameron, A. (1981). *Daughters of copper woman*. Adelphi.

Dolan, P., & Henwood, A. (2021). Five steps towards avoiding narrative traps in decision-making. *Frontiers in Psychology, 12*, 694032.

Timpe, K. (2021). *Disability and inclusive communities*. University of Notre Dame Press.

Timpe, K. (2023). "Disability and suffering" (with Hilary Yancey). In M. Grebe & J. Grossl (Eds.), *T&T Clark handbook of suffering and the problem of evil* (pp. 524–537). T&T Clark.

2

NO BUMP NO CARE

Core Problems in the First Trimester of Pregnancy

I. An Introduction

The first trimester of pregnancy is one of the most transformative periods in a woman's life, yet it is often lived in secrecy, hidden from coworkers and friends. Although these individuals could provide support to women experiencing this profound change, they are frequently the last to find out. As Patricia wrote in her story:

> I stood in the living room with a martini in one hand and the urine test stick in the other. I was aghast. . . . The martini became a symbol of my clear shock—I wouldn't have been drinking if I thought there was even a slim chance that I could be pregnant. . . . I had a consulting job that required me to travel and that week alone I flew to 3 different cities. A few weeks later the morning sickness came and I felt very vulnerable on planes and could no longer offer good excuses for not being able to participate in late sales dinners with clients. The slight smell of wine (or raw meat, or cigarettes, or gasoline, or certain people or foods) made me very nauseous. And I was always hungry and always so so so deeply exhausted. In a matter of 2 months, my usual rational, capable, overachieving self was so distant. I ate, slept and emoted, often irrationally, as if I was having PMS but on steroids. With the small amount of energy I had left, I started looking for a new job—one without travel and I did not tell them I was pregnant out of fear that they might not hire me if they knew.

As this part of her story illustrates, even though a support network should be in place to assist pregnant women, the beginning of this journey can be marked by

DOI: 10.4324/9781003490937-2

shock and isolation. For example, "The martini became a symbol of my clear shock". In this other story, Maren describes her pregnancy with these words:

> You caress your belly, you speak with it, at least I did constantly, more to reassure or calm myself than to actually interact, but anyway. . . . I never felt alone, I carried something/someone with me; she was always with me, which gave me a warm and confident feeling.

As you discover you are pregnant, you come into contact with the feeling that you are no longer alone, but at the same time you are isolated from the rest of people whose lives keep flowing as they used to. As Elliott wrote, "No one just woke up pregnant one day. As a gay man, the journey to parenthood was expensive, socially challenging, legally perilous and often very lonely". We are in ourselves, between ourselves and another. You are alone with your baby, but you and your baby are together "24 hours a day", trying to survive despite each other's limits (as Maren recounts). Kristeva describes this unique state as follows:

> Cells fuse, split, and proliferate; volumes grow, tissues stretch, and body fluids change rhythm, speeding up or slowing down. Within the body, growing as a graft, indomitable, there is an other. And no one is present, within that simultaneously dual and alien space, to signify what is going on. "It happens, but I'm not there". "I cannot realize it, but it goes on". Motherhood's impossible syllogism.
>
> *(1980, p. 237)*

As Kristeva describes in this passage, being pregnant is an impossible syllogism that challenges the Aristotelian logic of the principle of identity since the woman is A and not A at the same time (Bornemark, 2023). Because of the challenge that this (il)logical stretch puts on women's bodies, pregnancy can easily lead to a sense of alienation and emotional distress where they perceive their bodies as out of their control (Hodgkinson et al., 2014). Since they do not have control over all the changes occurring in their body, they delegate this control to institutionalized medical contexts that might transform the body of the woman into an object of care. Even if led by good intentions, the provider might transform the woman's body into an object that needs to meet parameters and standards in order to be cared for. As Nina recounts, "It took me some time to adjust to the fact that I needed medical assistance during my first birth".

Sometimes medical care becomes a way to delegate the responsibilities we have in interpreting the complexity of instincts and changes that we experience. The standards we look up to do not necessarily produce any meaning or sense of fulfillment for the pregnant woman but just, at times, bring a sense of calm and reassurance that everything unfolds according to the unwritten laws of nature.

Yet, this feeds in the detachment she might experience toward this incomprehensible body whose care she delegates to a doctor. Consequently, she might feed unrealistic expectations for her pregnancy, her postpartum body and her life after the delivery because these expectations are not rooted in her present embodied life but find their roots in a sort of curious machine that is out of her control. The result is that women might fall into the common emotional problem of postpartum mood disorders and depression (Clark et al., 2009). Despite the obvious hormonal and biological causes and the inevitable change in one's sense of identity, postpartum mood disorders and depression do not exclusively concern the period of time following the delivery of the baby, but they might find their roots in what precedes the delivery. In particular, the first trimester sets intentions and expectations that might shape the outcome of their future sense of self in the first months after the birth of the baby.

The feelings of alienation, resulting from this objectifying process, take women's agency away from their bodies, leading to a depressive state, which is dangerous for the mother, her partner and her new family. For this reason, in this chapter, I will focus on these three relevant emotional problems (alienation, objectification and loss of identity), especially as they set their roots in the first trimester of pregnancy, and I propose to use phenomenology as a mindful approach that can help the woman to be present to herself in the here-and-now if these problems arise and before medical interventions become necessary. In fact, it is in this first trimester that we can anticipate a pattern of behavior in relation to this "impossible syllogism" that might result in a dangerous sense of deep alienation (Cash & Szymanski, 1995). Unfortunately, given the secretive nature of this first trimester, little attention has been dedicated in the literature to the tremendous revolution that occurs in the woman's body during the first trimester, partly because it is caught in the debates concerning the legitimacy of abortion (which is beyond the current discussion) and partly because the first trimester does not show any qualitative difference to the external viewer. The first trimester of pregnancy seems a space that women have, as yet, failed to claim.

Hence, in the chapter, I will first point out the reasons why more attention should be paid to this trimester to avoid further development of depressive states. I will then individuate three core problems that characterize this phase. Finally, I will use phenomenology as a mindful approach to explain what these problems involve and what we can do to soften their effects on the emotional and physical balance of the pregnant woman.

II. The Forgotten First Trimester

Curiously, the first trimester of pregnancy did not receive as much attention in the literature as the other two trimesters (Adams & Lundquist, 2013). In the second trimester, apparent changes occur to the body that shake the notion of women's identity (Young, 1984) and its logic (Kristeva, 1980); the belly grows, the baby's kicks are noticeable and appetite increases. In the third trimester, women prepare to give birth to a new life that comes from them but is not them (Kristeva, 1980). For the first trimester, it is still unclear what the constituent elements are that characterize the initiation of the woman to this new life. In this lack of clarity, women often humor the expectations that are placed on them from close family and society. They pretend nothing is changing and keep carrying on with their lives. Nevertheless, despite its invisibility to others' eyes, these life-changing months strongly impact the woman's life and her partner(s). While everything remains the same for an external observer, the impact of this change might be strongly felt by the woman because of morning sickness, nausea, tender breasts, fatigue and other physical symptoms typical of this first trimester; yet, as in Patricia's story, her daily routine is largely expected to remain the same (work, family, health checks etc.). In the first trimester, the body has not visibly changed, but the woman knows and feels that some major change in her life is occurring—something that seems to be completely beyond her control. She does not feel the baby; she does not see herself differently, but everything within her demands that she behave differently: to slow down, to sleep more, to eat more regularly and to be more healthy.

The vulnerability (Boublil & Ferrarello, 2023; Quepons, 2020) of the woman's body at this stage is often compared to a general state of sickness[1]—and most insurances tend to treat it as such. In fact, as the 2002 WHO report shows, during this 12-week period, it is common to receive coverage for only one antenatal care visit[2] and no check-ups on the mental and physical health of the mother. This means that the woman is often left to herself and her ability to provide care for herself during this revolutionary moment of her life in which the risk of incurring complications is very high (Martonffy et al., 2012).

Making this first trimester an even more invisible and cumbersome condition is the legislation. To cite two examples: in the United States, it is only since the ACA in 2014 that early pregnancy (and pregnancy in general) has not been considered a condition; before the ACA, pregnancy was considered a preexisting condition, which meant insurers could decline or raise coverage prices for expecting mothers. Likewise, in Switzerland, miscarriage in the first trimester is still associated with illness as a complication of pregnancy.[3] Hence, "complications between the first week of pregnancy up until the 12th week are still classified as illnesses, so the insured person will still have to contribute towards treatment costs during this period of the pregnancy".[4]

As we know, vulnerability is not confined to the present moment; it also encompasses the horizon of possibilities that the woman envisions for herself (Quepons, 2020). In the first trimester, the woman is carrying a life that none can see and is compared to a sickness that can easily come and go at her physical, emotional and financial expenses. The progressive anticipations of "possible harm" and "emotional awareness of risk" are quite wide during this silent trimester.

Morning sickness, nausea and brain fog affect the emotional protentionality (Behnke, 2009) that previously allowed the woman's body to accomplish a normal routine of self-care and efficiency at work. This means that what was possible to plan in the future is now a source of anxiety, potential harm and fragility. In fact, as opposed to the second trimester, in which, generally, a burst of energy comes back to the woman's body, in the first trimester the woman's body feels often more tired (Martonffy et al., 2012)—what was easy to do before the pregnancy becomes questionable now: will I be able to meet with this client next week? Can I count on my strength to cook my food and bring it for lunch at work tomorrow? Moreover, in the first trimester, it often happens (Hasan et al., 2010) that occasional bleeding or light spotting transforms ordinary activities, such as using the restroom, into recurrent nightmares that are difficult to communicate to others. Any new blood stain becomes *deinos*—to use Sophocles—mysterious and terrifying at the same time. To quote from a forum of women who went through this experience:

> I know how you feel. I had bleeding my whole first trimester. It worried me to death, but it stopped and now I am 21 weeks and no issues.[5]
>
> I am 10 weeks + 4 days pregnant and over the weekend started bleeding, spotting at first on Sat, then once bright red when I wiped during the night and since then back to brown. All day yesterday had brown blood on and off, seemed to ease off by the evening but I've been up during the night and it's a lot heavier again. I've had 2 mc's <miscarriages> before this pregnancy and both times the bleeding started just like this so I am so scared that it's happening again. Rang the EPU yesterday but got straight through to one of the wards and the nurse who answered said with it being the weekend the clinic was closed and if I wanted to be seen by them I would have to go to A&E and get them to refer me for an appt. Spent nearly 5 hours there yesterday afternoon and they've got me an appt for a scan on Tuesday afternoon but I'm terrified that I'm going to miscarry again before then and I really don't think I can go through that again. What makes it worse is that I am still feeling horrendously sick, and my breasts are still feeling really heavy (not sore but I've not really had that anyway with this pregnancy) so I don't know what to think. Just cannot wait to get through today and tomorrow so I can find out what's happening. Had a little bleed at 5–6 weeks and was scanned then and again at 8 weeks and we saw baby with a good strong heartbeat, but I am just so scared that we're losing this one as well now.[6]

Despite their differences, these two excerpts manage to convey the sense of vulnerability and loneliness that accompany the daily lives of these two women during the first trimester. These are the feelings that often are sustained during the 12-week rule: pregnancy in the first trimester needs to remain a private affair (Olivier, 2012; Lindemann, 2019). Early pregnancy is a very delicate affair that, while absorbing the full attention of the woman, needs to remain separate (if not hidden) from her normal life and routine. In this secretive atmosphere, a sense of alienation can creep in to help the woman cope with her body during her daily life. It is likely at this moment that the woman starts alienating herself from her own body to cope with all the changing factors of her life. Given the high risk of miscarriage in the first trimester and the lack of testing during these weeks, women and their partners alienate themselves from their family, close friends and work life by keeping the big news secret. Warning the boss about the changes in their life would not be advisable because they might lose their job due to changes that might not be permanent. Yet, it is in this time that the woman's body (and her partner's) would need some additional care since the body is often more tired, as any smell can trigger nausea, brain fog makes self-expression less sharp, and lifting weights or standing on her feet is more challenging. As in Patricia's story, the first trimester of pregnancy meant for her to find a new job because she could not afford to travel as much as she used to while keeping secret the sense of nausea and tiredness she could feel at every meeting.

Conversely, it is mostly in the third trimester—when the woman can show proof of her change—that more care is conceded to her; one might think of the signs on public transportation advising passengers to offer the seat to women showing a bump. If the body does not show, care is not required. Yet, in this first trimester, the woman's body needs as much care as in the other trimesters because silencing the major revolution that occurs in these weeks might lead to a dangerous process of alienation, objectification and consequent loss of identity.

Whether this trimester ends in the delivery of a baby, a miscarriage or an abortion, this is a challenging moment in a woman's life and her partner(s) that, despite the requirements of the insurance codes discussed earlier, cannot be compared to flu or a general illness. In this time, more than in the other two trimesters, women and their partner(s) need support from colleagues at work, family and friends at home. Parenthetically, those more prone to break the 12-week rule and announce the pregnancy earlier are those women who previously suffered from miscarriage or pregnancy loss and are aware of how important it is to have a support network in place in case the first trimester evolves in a similar direction.[7]

I believe it is important to understand what kind of reality belongs to the lived experience of the first-trimester pregnancy in order to provide adequate support and a network of aid to women and their partners during this time. Hence, in the following sections, I will highlight at least three orders of problems that inform a woman's sense of vulnerability at this stage and offer a solution to these problems through a phenomenological approach that encourages mindful presence in regard to these issues.

II.1 Alienation, Objectification, Vitality: Three Problems

Alienation is one of the most relevant problems that might begin to occur in the first trimester of pregnancy. Its presence manifests itself in the discrepancy in what is affecting the woman's life: how she is asked to perform in her daily life and what she has been told to feel. For the woman, the ability to own the uniqueness of her own experience becomes like a mirage at this stage. The need to remain productive and carry on her life, the obsolete narrative of the maternal instincts and the maternal destiny for women (de Beauvoir, 1949; Hartsock, 1985; Kristeva, 1986) became the typical narrative the woman would hear when pregnant—and even before that. In fact, whether the pregnancy is going to end in a miscarriage, stillbirth, abortion or an alive birth, the first trimester of pregnancy will be a unique experience for the woman and her partners, which needs to acquire a meaning of its own. Reading personal stories from online forums shows the variety of experiences that might affect women at this stage:

> I suffer from anxiety and OCD. But since being pregnant my mental health has been so bad, obviously there is the rise in hormones but I'm to the point where I have multiple rage/anger or anxiety attacks a day, I've been under a lot of stress for so long and I'm just so so so worried that it will impact my baby, this is my first pregnancy and it's been so awful I hate not being able to control my emotions but I can't help but think I am making my baby suffer.[8]
>
> I have to admit, the night before my first scan at 12weeks I was awake and so nervous they would scan me and nothing would be there—that it had all been a mistake and I was just getting fat. I didn't really click in to "being pregnant" until about a month ago. Even before my 20 week scan I was still worried that I wasn't really pregnant. Sounds mental, I know.[9]

These two experiences are quite different, and even more qualitative differences would emerge if we read forums dedicated to in vitro fertilization pregnancies in the first trimester. Yet both experiences show how even if the pregnancy ends in a miscarriage, the woman might come to know what it means to have contractions and/or to reflect on her body in a new way; this experience must become meaning. Even if the experience of "horror, of invasive parasitical entity growths" (Hartsock, 1985, p. 28) might arise as a powerful distancing effect that would separate the woman from her own body, this feeling of horror must become meaning. Unfortunately, the hospitals hardly ever offer support for women in their first trimester. Consequently, most of these confusing feelings do not find a way to become organized emotions and eventually express themselves in meanings.[10] Women losing their baby at 12 weeks to natural miscarriages are asked to get over it as if that was just the flu, as Alison Stone recounts in the webinar on Being Born I organized for my university.[11] This does not take into account the truths of the body. What it means to see the blood and tissue material of your fetus on your underwear, the contractions that accompany this ejection and the emotional and physical exhaustion that follow the event. As Marzia recounts, we might feel "broken":

> When I disclosed my miscarriage at eight weeks to my mother, she suggested that I might be somehow broken. Such responses, though hurtful, intensified my pervasive feeling of inadequacy in procreation. I have encountered many women who have gone through miscarriages, ectopic pregnancies, and stillbirths, and we all felt somewhat broken, with deep emotional wounds.

The overall point is that the event of the pregnancy that characterizes this first trimester is unique, and this uniqueness will remain a benchmark in the life of the woman, partner(s) involved and future family. The unique feelings experienced by women during this time cannot find their unique narratives in external points of view; they generate a new horizon of meanings that need to be unpacked. Unfortunately, the collective narratives available to unpack these meanings are quite narrow, and so is the time the woman has available to recover from a pregnancy and reflect on its meaning. That is why it is important to be present in these moments characterizing the first trimester and avoid the temptation to alienate oneself from them by using a mindful approach to these new events.

Connected to the former, the second problem observable in the first trimester refers to the objectification of the body and the consequent loss of meaning. Husserl refers to the phenomenology of pregnancy as one of the case limits of lived experience (Husserl, 1973a, p. 597). It is a case limit because the other is intended (Seinsinn) by the woman and her partner(s) as an emotional content of her life, but it also has its own being (Sosein) (Husserl, 1976, text #6). Even though the woman's body is the presupposition for the empathetic connection that we can establish with the embryo for the constitution of the other and the world (Husserl, 1983, text 16), we cannot fully intend this being as its own being since it is at the very stage of forming itself in the womb of the mother. Hence, the woman's body becomes this opaque, inexplicable, self-moving object over which the woman might feel she has lost any control (Hodgkinson et al., 2014). As we saw earlier, in the first trimester, the emotional and physical health of the mother is not yet properly tested, and most of the education is left to self-help forums, which often contribute to the growth of anxiety (Schetter & Tanner, 2012). In this void, the woman might find it easier to let anxiety, mood changes and other new states of mind slip into passivity, accepting them as a matter of fact without questioning their meaning and finding the sense that they hold in her life. A form of disembodiment might arise that would lead to even more unstable moods and difficult self-care. She might delegate entirely the care of her body to doctors and medical personnel.

There is a third problem, as a consequence of the previous two. The first trimester is phenomenologically a very complex phase during the arc of pregnancy because it might be draining, emotionally and physically. It can significantly lower the feelings of vitality, which, during and after the pregnancy, might trigger a loss of identity and depressive states. Moreover, since one out of three women does not arrive at the end of the pregnancy, it might be that on top of the physical and emotional fatigue accompanying the lowered feelings of vitality, the woman would have to cope with psychological distress and a sense of guilt and relief caused by the abrupt interruption of the pregnancy. A corollary to this third point is the fact that when the first trimester starts going wrong, building trust with healthcare professionals becomes even more difficult. In fact, when symptoms of a miscarriage occur, the woman might have to act out of emergency, and it is difficult for her to schedule an appointment with her regular obstetrician/gynecologist. Hence, it is whoever is available in the ER room that becomes the main way to take care of the pregnant woman. It is at this stage that the problem of interoperability and the free flow of data inherent to the new technologies and privacy legislation in use by hospitals become painfully present (Conn, 2016). The doctors will know only what they are seeing at the moment. It will be up to the patient to give the full picture to the visiting doctor. First, this involves the risk of omitting important information, and second, the increased risk of anxiety due to the chaos that the experience generates.

III. Mindfulness and Phenomenology as a Way to Approach These Problems

While I do not have space to develop a solution for this latter corollary problem, I will use phenomenology to describe the former three issues in order to find mindful solutions for them. As it concerns the connection between phenomenology and mindfulness (Ferrarello & Hadjioannou, 2024a, 2024b), it can very briefly be said that some consider phenomenology as a way to achieve mindfulness (Stone & Zahavi, 2021), while others view phenomenology and mindfulness as equivalent psychological resources to provide for human well-being (Walach, 2021). Because both phenomenology and mindfulness involve paying attention to the present experience with a specific attitude (Lundh, 2020), I believe that both can offer support to individuals experiencing emotional problems (Guendelman et al., 2017; Lutz et al., 2015). Hence, in what follows, I will use phenomenological descriptions of the three problems mentioned earlier to foster mindful presence in cases where problems that may impact the emotional well-being of the woman may arise.

III.1 Finding One's Own Voice

The problem of alienation can be interpreted through the lenses of collective intentionality. Husserl's volumes on intersubjectivity (, 1973bHusserl, 1973a,

1973c) and Stein's (1917) study on collective emotions open the dialogue on how an individual's intentions and emotions are expressed and recognized in the collective society. Searle's 1990 (but also 1995) paper represents the baptism of this notion, which elucidates how individuals' intentions and accordingly their lived experiences engage with the life-world not only in an individual way but also in a collective way. The collective intention that describes the connecting bridge between individuals and their shared world should not be seen as a summation of individual intentionality and reciprocal attitudes but as irreducibly collective.

According to Stein's account of communal experiences (Gemeinschaftserlebnisse), "the relation between individual and communal experiences is constitution, not summation" (Stein, Beitrage, 211). In society, an individual's intentions can merge with those of others to such an extent that, once these intentions are fully realized, we may lose sight of our original purpose or goals. As mentioned earlier, this form of alienation is often caused by the divergence between the societal pre-constituted meanings that apply to the woman who discovers she is pregnant in her first trimester and the actual experience that this same woman undergoes in those 12 weeks. A woman who is still learning to understand her body and what she feels about these enormous transformations might find it easier to lean on meanings that are preconstituted by society. Instead of trying to connect with her own intentions and the meanings they are trying to reach, she identifies with a sense that has been pre-organized in the society. An example of preconstituted meaning might be the usual belief that the first trimester is not a big transformative moment of a woman's life. If the pregnancy does not continue, the woman can come back easily to her life. In this pre-constituted sense, many women found a sense of alienation that significantly slows down the process of healing.

In our society, we often encounter ourselves and others in a pre-reflective attitude and engage in a pre-reflective constitution of collective meanings and values. This means that we do not have time to know what is happening to us. The meaning always arises afterwards when we make time to reflect on what that lived experience meant for us. Meanings are the product of a personal reflection on what we experienced. If we do not find time to reflect on the lived experience and generate our unique meanings, we end up borrowing these meanings from collective ones pre-constituted in society. This often applies to simple habits or activities—what it means for us to have breakfast, to go to work, to get dressed. We often need to lean on pre-constituted meanings to make certain simple choices of our day faster. More complex is the application of this to pregnancy. For example, the sense of happiness that a woman might feel when discovering she is pregnant changes according to the context and societal norms in which this discovery occurs. If a single woman discovers she is pregnant in a conservative and tight Hasidic community in New York City, she would attach to that experience a very different pre-reflective meaning when compared to a woman making this same discovery in a more liberal Jewish family living in the same city. The fulfillment of meaning expected from that same lived experience would vary greatly according to the normative patterns implied in that collective compound.

If a woman is expecting a baby before having a husband in a Hasidic community, it means that a set of rules has been broken and that the first trimester in which the pregnancy does not yet show is a journey of misery and anguish in which the woman must decide what to do. The sense of kindness and care women are capable of having toward themselves during those first 12 weeks of pregnancy can be strongly influenced by the meanings and values pre-assigned to that experience, which result from the environment in which they grew up, worked and lived. If pregnancy without a husband is considered a sin, it will require a strong interpretive effort to propose an alternative meaning; or if a pregnancy loss is compared to flu, it will take strong emotional energy to find the space to properly mourn that loss and let their grief unfold (Swanson, 1999; Green et al., 2009).

What Heidegger calls "the habits, customs, and publicness of everydayness" (1999, p. 103) represent the result and the starting point of this co-constituting framework of habitual meanings in which we are pre-reflectively engaged and where we encounter each other in the definition of what is appropriate or inappropriate, legitimate or illegitimate. If it is considered illegitimate to feel scared of being pregnant because every life must be a blessing, it might be possible that this pre-reflective feeling will be silenced and probably transformed into a less understandable behavior. The implied normative pattern of behaviors nurtured by the responses that are repeatedly given to the network of feelings, emotions and sensations connected to certain lived experiences influences our personal responses and personal constitution of meanings. If we know mourning a miscarriage is unusual in our social surroundings, we might take the habit to suppress that feeling and maybe become judgmental toward one's own and others' sense of tenderness when it arises.

III.2 Thinking as Usual

In this sense, the first trimester of pregnancy throws the woman into a new system of habits while being still connected to the old ones that pace her routine life. Everything in her body is changing, but her life-world still expects her to be the same. It is within this life-world that the woman is embedded and produces the meanings that guide her choices, and yet this world might become at some point insufficient to resonate with the changes that her body is demanding from her. There are new epistemological and axiological orientation schemes that need to be rebuilt and meanings to be assigned. It takes mindful presence and phenomenological reflection over the new lived experience to rebuild a new system of habits resonating with what the woman is truly becoming. Without this presence, the pregnant woman becomes a stranger in her own body and accordingly alienates herself from her own life. For this reason, she needs to break with the system of habitualities (Schutz, 1945; Husserl, 1976) that she used to follow and find new ones that are her own.

> The discovery that things in <her> new surroundings look quite different from what <she> expected them to be at home is frequently the first shock to the stranger's confidence in the validity of her habitual "thinking as usual".
>
> *(Schutz, 1945, p. 99)*

In the first trimester, the woman and her partner need to challenge the validity of "habitual thinking as usual" in order to let a new pre-reflective layer of collective intention unfold and be integrated with the previous ones. Going out for a run, eating junk food, staying up late—these are examples of simple habitualities that might need to be revised as they will encounter unusual effects on the woman's body. Feeling scared, inadequate and confused are more complex and yet common emotions that might become part of the new system of habitualities, which the woman might feel reluctant to accept based on her upbringing if she was told that becoming a mother would be the most natural fulfillment of her life. This specific set of integrations—which seem very small at first—is a difficult goal to achieve and is not often sufficiently thematized and understood. Its recognition shakes in small foundational ways the continuity of the identity of the woman. Yet the shakeup is necessary to guarantee continuity with her sense of identity.

Emotional reality results from the ongoing co-presence and co-participation of the correlated subject and its object, noesis and noema, agent and its surroundings. The passivity of our vegetative state holds an important part of our intentionality, whose responsibility we rarely claim and whose motivations and contents we rarely question because our subjectivity is not yet there. Nevertheless, this intentionality is equally responsible for the constitution of a pre-reflective layer that surrounds us and generates the sense of harmony we feel with the environment. We are this pre-reflective intentionality, and its fundamental changes have the power to shake our sense of self in a way that seems almost invisible to us. How the woman responds to nausea, what it means for her to gain/lose weight and how the brain fog impacts her working life are pre-reflective states that strongly influence the primordial and pre-reflective roots of her intentionality and the (in)congruency with which it manifests in our collective emotions. "Primordiality is a system of impulses" (Husserl, 1975) that, in a pre-reflective way, constitutes the reality of the individual before its ego-center and subjectivity is called into existence. It is then of the utmost importance for the woman to connect with the primordiality of her own impulses in order to build a consistent core of pre-reflective habits, which grounds her emotional reality in a way that is consistent with her new system of impulses; this connection would channel a coherent communication with the social world and its expectations. Being mindfully aware of the bodily and resulting emotional individual changes paves the way to being part of a coherent collective intentionality in a way that is consistent with one's own intentionality as an individual.

III.3   My Body, an Object

A second class of problems that occur during the first trimester of pregnancy relates to the objectification of the woman's body. These problems mostly refer to the difficulty the woman encounters when addressing the changes she goes through, especially in relation to the interplay between the living body (Leib) and the organic body (Koerper). For the sake of the woman's health, it would be good to avoid dichotomizing views of her body as split with an unknown otherness (Kristeva, 1980; Young, 1984) or stuck in an impossible syllogism (Kristeva, 1980; Bornemark, 2023). Being able to mindfully adapt to the change of energy, strength and the possibility of functioning is strongly beneficial to the emotional and physical well-being of the woman. As Patricia writes:

> At first his <my husband's> excitement and clear welcoming of this baby is what made it possible for me to embrace what was happening even a little bit. It also made it possible for me to handle all that was needing to change in my life and in my body, none of which felt comfortable or easy. I was feeling completely overwhelmed and taken over by the experience on every front.

Our main source for the constitution of meanings comes from the way in which our body experiences life: if we live with our body as something disconnected from us because of the pregnancy, then a sense of disembodiment and consequent mood disorders and depression might arise.

The ways in which we can refer to our body are numerous. I can consider my body as a machine that brings me wherever I want. I can look at it as a burden that prevents me from doing what I desire. It can be my business card through which others can like me. Phenomenology encourages us to see our body as our center of orientation. This means that the body is not a separate entity from me that I consider a burden or a tool according to circumstances, but it is what I can be when I am living. When the woman is in her first trimester, she lives in a body that is going through rapid and sudden changes. Opposing oneself against these changes in order to keep pace with work or to hide the pregnancy from one's own community becomes a draining exercise that leads her to not live in her own body—hence, disembodiment, alienation and emotional exhaustion. Instead of being an agentic subject, the body becomes the object of everyone else's interest.

The living biological body (Koerper) establishes contact with the living body (Leib) at each movement. If I decide to touch my belly, this little movement can create a meaningful healing connection with myself and the life to come. As Maren wrote, she touched her belly as a way to reassure herself that everything was going well.

It is this primal kinesthetic realization that makes life meaningful. My body understands that "I can" move and make choices; this allows me to know that I am (alive). My living body (Leib) tells me that I am a living biological body (Koerper) that has the potential to do numerous things in life. What happens in the first trimester is that the "I can" starts changing drastically. Adjusting to what is truly achievable in the interplay between Leib and Koerper is an exercise of patience and mindful presence that is necessary to undertake to avoid the temptation to become fully Koerper and lose the connection with the Leib. This means being able to see and explore, through mindfulness, meditation and/or enactivism, where the woman's Koerper is in the given moment and which functioning (Leistung) the living body (Leib) can initiate in that given moment. This, of course, requires humility for the woman to accept that she no longer knows her body and must become acquainted with the new range of possibilities at her disposal. Missing this opportunity of self-exploration would transform her body into a biological object whose care is mostly left to doctors and other figures of authority. Since we are embodied beings, we need to stay in our body, especially when rapid changes invest it. This embodiment allows us to be aware of the wide array of possibilities that our living and biological body offers us in order to fully live our life. The joy of being alive comes exactly from the awareness of these possibilities.

III.4   Disembodied Beings

It might happen that when discovering one is pregnant, the woman's mind travels much faster than her body. We think more than we can feel. We get stuck in our heads or in the heads of people who tend to always see us in a certain way. We mimic what we think we should be, according to our preconceptions or the expectations of the family and friends around us. It is in these moments that we get further and further away from what the here-and-now of what our Leib indicates for us in that moment.

Our living body (Leib) is in fact our bodily compass, or as phenomenological philosophy calls it, our center of orientation that tells us at each given moment what matters here and now. I am sitting on this chair while I am writing. I am taking a walk. I am feeling my body in good shape.

Our living body (Leib) is there to remind us of what we are in that moment and what we can do in that moment with what we are. It is our center of being.

However, it happens that when our mind thinks too much and feels too little, we get more in tune with the expectations of others (doctors, family, partners) and suppress the needs of our living body—something similar to the dynamic of collective intentionality I was pointing to above. We almost think that what our body has to say is superfluous and out of place, and we pay attention only to these disembodied thoughts.

Yet, in the long run, whether the pregnancy ends in a delivery or not, disembodied thoughts generate a disembodied being, and a disembodied being does not have a body to put into practice the projects or ideas that come to mind. If we let disembodiment take over, we risk becoming zombies, capable of repeating the same tasks but unable to truly enjoy life and what it offers us. As Camilla writes:

> I did have some "crisis" with my body because I was not very good at holding my urine in some situations, and this bothered me and created embarrassment for myself. However, the more serious "problems" began after Mia was born. The first three months were a nightmare. I lived in a state of discomfort because I didn't feel happy. It's hard to explain, but looking back now, I almost can't believe it because things have completely changed. At first, I saw Mia, but I couldn't completely rejoice in the fact that she was here. Plus, I had an unplanned cesarean section, which destabilized me a lot because of the scar that I still have difficulty seeing as something positive.
>
> My husband even thought I had the so-called postpartum depression, and this belief made me even more upset because I was certain of what I was feeling and that it was just a momentary feeling, as it turned out to be.

When we are disembodied, we feel our mood is low, and every action we want to initiate seems the hardest to accomplish. We cannot take pleasure even from the most evident events in our lives. Our body does not respond to our expectations; we are not in sync with it. Consequently, instead of being instrumental to our functioning, it becomes a burden we carry around with ourselves during the day. This happens when for too long we have been feeling detached from it because, in the case of pregnancy, it is fat and cumbersome. Hence, it is even more important during the first trimester to be able to connect with one's own body and be able to feel the changes that the organic body is going through, independent of whether they are considered acceptable or not from our past self and the community we belong to.

III.5   Low Vitality

The third class of problems I focus on in this chapter is the loss of identity that might already occur in the first 12 weeks of pregnancy. In this sense, it is important to see how feelings of vitality impact the emotional and physical fatigue that might characterize the first trimester of pregnancy. Else Voigtländer connects the feeling of vitality to the feeling of the self and of one's own value. Being able to feel oneself and one's own value generates a sense of awareness for oneself and the possibility of our own being in the world that otherwise would be missing (Voigtländer, 1910, p. 54). For this reason, feelings of the self are considered as vital feelings that indicate our capability to be in the world and achieve our goals in it; per extension, feelings of the self are necessary for the biological body (Koerper) to connect with the living body (Leib) and for one's own intention to be expressed with clarity in the intentionality of the collective.

This loss is not necessarily connected solely to the biological body and its changes. As Elliott wrote:

> The journey to this juncture was impacted by strife and joy, challenge and ease, sacrifice and awakenings to multiple new identities. This time began to shift the core of my identity in ways that I could not articulate at the time.

The multiple changes characterizing the beginning of motherhood, especially in the first trimester of pregnancy, derive partly from the sudden questioning of our sense of self as expressed in the reduced capabilities of the body (both as Koerper and as Leib) and in a lower intentional energy to bring to determination all the new meanings that the new bodily life presents to the woman. In a private conversation with Elliott, who as a man never experienced pregnancy, he told me how his practical concrete life changed upon the arrival of his first child. His way of spending money, completing chores and working had to take a different direction, and this is still changing as his children are growing and becoming more independent.

In one word, life, in the preparation for motherhood, the organic life starts flowing too fast and in all new directions—this leaves the woman (or any primary caregiver) little time to feel her new self and to make sense of it. These changes might severely drain the feeling of the self because the body becomes literally less capable of achieving goals that up to that moment were connected to basic well-being and self-fulfillment, such as going for a run or being able to accomplish a project with punctuality. Accordingly, self-awareness is difficult to develop because the self that the woman was used to is embodied in a center of orientations that is new in many of its aspects and vulnerable for most of the time. The level of pleasure or pain (Voigtländer, 1910, p. 37) that we can achieve is completely different to what the woman was used to in accordance with her previous successes and failures.

In his *Formalism in Ethics and Non-formal Ethics of Values* (1973), Scheler describes vital feelings as those feelings in which you feel tired, ill or alive relating to vital values such as being honorable or morally weak. In that sense, vital feelings are the feelings that the lived body perceives when it is conscious of what the biological body is capable of. For example, especially in the first trimester, when the chances of a miscarriage are still very high, it might be that feeling vitally low and emotionally drained—although a life is being formed in the womb—is connected to an implicit moral judgment that the woman reserves toward "her" questionable capability to successfully carry the child until the end of term. The woman might question her bodily skills and put a tremendous responsibility over her body despite no responsibility being imputable to that biological process (Lok & Neugebauer, 2007). The value feelings connected to these bodily feelings are expressed in the lived body in ambiguous terms; it is not possible to localize them as we would do for sensations such as pleasure or pain because these feelings do not have an actual extension in the body. As Scheler puts it, "A feeling of comfort and its opposite, e.g., health and illness, fatigue and vigor, cannot be determined in terms of localization of certain organs" (Scheler, 1973, p. 338).

The woman feels a drastically different kind of vitality in her body even if everything still looks the same. In vital feelings, she can feel herself in a sort of intuitive and axiological apprehension of her lived body. This means that she assigns a positive or negative value to what her instincts can perceive in that moment. It is not about feeling comfortable or in a good mood, but it is about the ability to feel herself—that is, as a unitary center connected to the multiple rays projected by these feelings (Scheler, 1973, p. 339). The "myself" is here understood in terms of a unitary consciousness of her lived body (Leib), which Scheler refers to as the "lived-body-ego" (Leibich). For this reason, it is important from the first trimester of pregnancy to start paying mindful attention to one's own vital feelings because they can offer the key to describing the functional and intentional character of our experience so that we can get closer to our feeling of self. This would allow the woman to retain her self-worth and her sense of identity. In these feelings, "we feel our life itself, its 'growth,' its 'decline,' its 'illness,' its 'health,' and its 'future'; i.e., something is given to us in this feeling" (Scheler, 1973, p. 340). They can "evidentially indicate the vital meaning of the value of events and processes within and outside my body; they can indicate, as it were, their vital 'sense'" (Scheler, 1973, p. 341). They indicate values related to life in our body as a "system of signs for the changing states of life-processes" (Scheler, 1973, p. 341). As Scheler puts it, "They point to the value of what is coming, not to the value of what is present" (Scheler, 1973, p. 342). Accordingly, to prevent the sense of loss of identity, it might be useful to examine how the vital feelings experienced in the first trimester can anticipate what is going to develop throughout and after the pregnancy.

IV. Conclusion

In this chapter, I have presented three core problems that might already appear in the first trimester of pregnancy: alienation, objectification and loss of identity, which might cause emotional distress for the woman (or any primary caregiver) and further develop into depressive states. In this chapter, I have indicated the kind of mindful approach we can use to reduce the impact of these problems.

1. As it concerns alienation, mindful presence should be paid to the construction of a new system of habitualities so that the woman can own her unique voice in relation to the basic experiences she is investing in her new body. Accordingly, it is of the utmost importance for the woman to connect with the primordiality of her own impulses in order to build a consistent core of pre-reflective habits that ground her emotional reality in a way that is more consistent with her new system of pre-reflective experiences. This would facilitate the constitution of meanings she can attribute to her experience, as well as a coherent communication with her surrounding social world. Being mindfully present to the body and aware of the changes it goes through paves the way to being part of a coherent voice within the collective intentions that make our sense of community.

2. The second problem is connected to objectification, which leads to a severe loss of meaning in relation to what the living body can still do. The impossible syllogism for which the woman is both herself and another at the same time might strongly disrupt the empathetic connection that the woman can establish with her own body and her baby. Being able to be present to one's own body and the identity and alterity that it carries simultaneously is certainly a challenging emotional task. For this reason, I suggested that women in this situation pay mindful attention to the daily interplay that is truly achievable between Leib and Koerper according to the new balance of their bodies. This means being able to see and explore where the woman's Koerper is in the given moment and which functioning (Leistungen) the living body (Leib) can initiate in that given moment. Of course, this requires humility from the woman to accept that she no longer knows her own body and must become reacquainted with the new range of possibilities at her disposal.

3. The third problem, connected with the previous two, implies a loss of identity, which is connected to feelings of vitality. From the first trimester of pregnancy, it is important to start paying mindful attention to one's own vital feelings because they can offer the key to describing the functional and intentional qualities of our experience. They can offer us the map to connect with our feeling of self and understand where we stand in relation to our life. This would allow the woman not to lose the sense of her self-worth and with it her sense of identity because, although not localizable, our vital feelings are capable of pointing out to us the value of what is present in our experience.

In general, instead of paying attention to women's emotional problems *post factum* as an exclusively post-partum problem, it is helpful to pay attention to the potential areas of risk already visible from the first trimester. In this chapter,

I have highlighted how mindful presence and phenomenological observation of at least three areas of the lived experience characterizing the first 12 weeks of pregnancy might be beneficial to the emotional well-being of the woman and her partner(s).

Notes

1 https://www.unicef.org/parenting/pregnancy-milestones/first-trimester
2 https://www.who.int/publications/i/item/9789241549912
3 According to Swiss Federal Law on Health Insurance (FLHI), before 1 March 2014, under the old law, miscarriage at any stage of pregnancy was counted as "illness" (as were all lesser pregnancy complications), and so one's normal franchise/excess/deductible applied.
4 https://www.ch.ch/en/pregnancy-health-insurance-covers/
5 https://community.whattoexpect.com/forums/what-to-expect-general-message-board/topic/anyone-experience-bleeding-early-on-and-still-had-a-healthy-pregnancy.html
6 https://www.netmums.com/coffeehouse/becoming-mum-ttc-64/early-pregnancy-signs-symptoms-537/660683-terrified-10-weeks-pregnant-bleeding-again.html
7 https://www.smh.com.au/lifestyle/life-and-relationships/it-was-all-ripped-away-the-cruel-irony-of-the-12-week-rule-20191011-p52zzd.html
8 beyondblue.org
9 https://www.ohbaby.co.nz/forum/what-was-your-first-trimester-like_topic36404.html
10 This often leads to developing disorganized attachments to their babies for women who suffered from pregnancy loss in the first trimester (Bakermans-Kranenburg MJ, Schuengel C, van Ijzendoorn MH., 1999).
11 https://www.youtube.com/watch?v=n5I7sQ4h0zo&ab_channel=SusiFerrarello

References

Adams, S. L., & Lundquist, C. R. (Eds.). (2013). *Coming to life: Philosophies of pregnancy, childbirth, and mothering.* Fordham University Press.

Behnke, E. A. (2009). Bodily protentionality. *Husserl Studies, 25*(3), 185–217.

Boublil, E., & Ferrarello, S. (2023). *The vulnerability of the human world.* Springer.

Cash, T., & Szymanski, M. (1995). The development and validation of the body-image ideals questionnaire. *Journal of Personal Assessment, 64*(3), 466–477.

Clark, A., Skouteris, H., Wertheim, E., Paxton, S., & Milgrom, J. (2009). The relationship between depression and body dissatisfaction across pregnancy and the postpartum a prospective study. *Journal of Health Psychology, 14*(1), 27–35.

Conn, J. (2016, January 23). Seeking a solution for patient record matching. *Modern Healthcare.* Retrieved May 3, 2016, from http://www.modernhealthcare.com/article/20160123/MAGAZINE/301239980

de Beauvoir, S. (1949). *The second sex* (H. M. Parshley, Ed. and Trans.). Vintage Book.

Ferrarello, S., & Hadjioannou, C. (2024a). *The Routledge handbook of phenomenology and mindfulness.* Routledge.

Ferrarello, S., & Hadjioannou, C. (2024b). Phenomenology and mindfulness. *The Journal of Humanistic Psychology.*

Green, R. S., Malig, B., Windham, G. C., Fenster, L., Ostro, B., & Swan, S. (2009). Residential exposure to traffic and spontaneous abortion. *Environmental Health Perspectives, 117*(12), 1939–1944.

Guendelman, S., Medeiros, S., & Rampes, H. (2017). Mindfulness and emotion regulation: Insights from neurobiological, psychological, and clinical studies. *Frontiers in Psychology, 8*, 220.

Hartsock, N. (1985). *Money, sex, and power: Toward a feminist historical materialism.* Northeastern University Press.

Hasan, R., Baird, D. D., Herring, A. H., Olshan, A. F., Jonsson Funk, M. L., & Hartmann, K. E. (2010). Patterns and predictors of vaginal bleeding in the first trimester of pregnancy. *Annals of Epidemiology, 20*(7), 524–531.

Heidegger, M. (1999). *Ontologie: Hermeneutik der Faktizität* (J. Van Buren, Trans.). Indiana University Press.

Hodgkinson, E. L., Smith, D. M., & Wittkowski, A. (2014). Women's experiences of their pregnancy and postpartum body image: A systematic review and meta-synthesis. *BMC Pregnancy and Childbirth, 14*, 330.

Husserl, E. (1973a). *Zur Phänomenologie der Intersubjektivität. Texte aus dem Nachlass. Dritter Teil. 1929–35.* [*On the phenomenology of intersubjectivity. Texts from the estate. Third part. 1929–35.*] (I. Kern, Ed.). Martinus Nijhoff.

Husserl, E. (1973b). *Zur Phänomenologie der Intersubjektivität. Texte aus dem Nachlass. Zweiter Teil. 1921–28* (I. Kern, Ed.). Martinus Nijhoff.

Husserl, E. (1973c). *Zur Phänomenologie der Intersubjektivität* (I. Kern, Ed.). Martinus Nijhoff.

Husserl, E. (1975). *Experience and judgment.* Northwestern Press.

Husserl, E. (1976). *The crisis of European sciences and transcendental philosophy. An introduction to phenomenology* (W. Biemel, Ed.). Martinus Nijhoff.

Husserl, E. (1983). *Ideas pertaining to a pure phenomenology and to a phenomenological philosophy* (F. Kersten, Ed.). Martinus Nijhoff.

Kristeva, J. (1980). Motherhood according to Bellini. In T. Gora, A. Jardine, & L. S. Roudiez (Eds.), *Desire in language: A semiotic approach to literature and art* (pp. 3–17). Columbia University Press. (Original work published 1977).

Kristeva, J. (1986). Women's time. In T. Moi (Ed.), *The Kristeva reader* (pp. 187–213). Columbia University Press.

Lindemann, K. (2019). *The 12-week pregnancy rule makes the pain of miscarriage worse.* https://www.theguardian.com/commentisfree/2019/oct/07/12-week-pregnancy-rule-miscarriage-shame-failure

Lok, I. H., & Neugebauer, R. (2007). Psychological morbidity following miscarriage. *Best Practices Research in Clinical Obstetrics Gynaecology, 21*(2), 229–247.

Lundh, L. G. (2020). Experimental phenomenology in mindfulness research. *Mindfulness, 11*, 493–506.

Lutz, A., Jha, A., Dunne, J. D., & Saron, C. D. (2015). Investigating the phenomenological matrix of mindfulness-related practices from a neurocognitive perspective. *American Psychology, 70*, 632–658.

Martonffy, A. I., Rindfleisch, K., Lozeau, A. M., & Potter, B. (2012). First trimester complications. *Primary Care, 39*(1), 71–82.

Olivier, K. (2012). *Knock me down. Knock me up.* Columbia University Press.

Quepons, I. (2020). Vulnerability and trust. *PhaenEx, 13*(2), 1–10.

Scheler, M. (1973). *Formalism in ethics and non-formal ethics of values.* Northwestern University Press.

Schetter D. C., & Tanner, L. (2012). Anxiety, depression and stress in pregnancy: Implications for mothers, children, research, and practice. *Current Opinion in Psychiatry, 25*(2), 141–148.

Schutz, A. (1945). The homecomer. *American Journal of Sociology, 50*(5), 369–376.

Searle, J. R. (1990). Collective intentions and actions. In P. Cohen, J. Morgan, & M. E. Pollack (Eds.), *Intentions in communication.* Bradford Books, MIT Press.

Stein, E. (1917). *Zur Problem der Einfühlung, Waisenhouse*. Max Niemeyer.
Stone, O., & Zahavi, D. (2021). Phenomenology and mindfulness. *Journal of Consciousness Studies, 28*(3–4), 158–185.
Swanson, K. M. (1999). Effects of caring, measurement, and time on miscarriage impact and women's well-being. *Nursing Research, 48*(6), 288–298.
Voigtländer, E. (1910). *Über die Typen des Selbstgefühls*. R. Voigtländer Verlag.
Walach, H. (2021). Mindfulness is phenomenology, phenomenology is mindfulness. *Constructivist Foundations, 16*(2), 236–237.
Young, I. M. (1984). Pregnant embodiment: Subjectivity and alienation. *The Journal of Medicine and Philosophy: A Forum for Bioethics and Philosophy of Medicine, 9*(1), 45–62.

3
BREASTFEEDING IN WONDERLAND

Exploring (Dis)Embodied Experience

I. Nobody Tells You . . .

"Nobody tells you how hard breastfeeding is"—this is a sentiment I have often heard from my clients, friends and others involved in this book. Breastfeeding is a lifestyle choice that some women decide to embrace without knowing ahead of time its implications. Society often idealizes breastfeeding as a celestial experience where the woman and baby peacefully connect. While this is certainly part of the experience, it overlooks the sleepless nights needed to maintain milk supply, the risk of mastitis and severe infections from clogged or engorged milk ducts, the excruciating pain and overwhelming guilt a mother feels when she must return to work and pump to continue feeding her baby, and the drastic reduction in mobility to allow the baby to latch on demand or to pump milk. As Maren wrote:

> When you are breast feeding, you are all body, you, your needs, or person are not important anymore. You also feel extremely insecure as you do not know (yet) what the baby needs or wants, what to do. You feel guilty and a real loser, if the breastfeeding doesn't work out or you do not get your baby or your body in the right drinking positions (it takes in general more than week before this technically and bodily works out, and most women give up in despair when they do not receive proper supervision by nurses or midwives). Bodily, breast feeding is a very intense experience, in the positive and the negative. Before the milk is ready, it mostly hurts, you have inflammations, your breasts get hard as stone, you get a fever, while breastfeeding it mostly hurts (for many women) in the beginning, nipples are sore and need to be treated etc. Also, it

DOI: 10.4324/9781003490937-3

feels like your breast are no longer part of you, but of a strange new body in service of feeding your child. They change in form and quantity to such an extent that you do not even feel ashamed if someone would see them in public (while breastfeeding) because they do in no way remind you of your former old bodily self.

As Maren writes, when a woman breastfeeds, the body becomes the center of everything. She becomes the body in all its primal needs and functions. She is this body in all its resources and limits. Unfortunately, numerous physical problems can arise when a mother, absorbed by her duties, does not take sufficient care of herself. These include back pain from hunching to hold the baby close to her chest, carpal tunnel syndrome from frequently lifting and moving the baby, cramping due to the release of hormones like oxytocin during breastfeeding, which helps the uterus shrink back to its original size, and osteoporosis, as breastfeeding can lead to a significant loss of bone mass unless the mother maintains a healthy diet and exercise regimen, which can be challenging during the early years of the baby's life. Until life places you in such a situation, either as a male partner of a breastfeeding woman or as a breastfeeding woman herself, it is very difficult to comprehend all the upheavals associated with this practice (Doucet, 2006). Even the challenging decision regarding breastfeeding requires consideration from both the baby and the parents. Sometimes, the baby struggles to latch, or the mother might lack the energy to choose breastfeeding over bottle feeding. In some cases, either the mother or the baby may be unable to make breastfeeding possible. These situations can create anxiety, guilt, shame and emotional problems that might be eased through some counseling or psychotherapy (McFadden et al., 2019). However, a new mother in a typical-income family often lacks the time and financial resources to afford psychotherapy. As a result, she may have to cope with this sense of guilt while also learning how to be a mother and understand her new baby's character. If both baby and mother manage to overcome these challenges and successfully breastfeed, the real work of breastfeeding then begins.

I.1 Nature Says: "Breast Is Best"

With a conservative estimate of 1,800 hours a year, breastfeeding is a full-time job that women take on as "natural" primary caregivers of their infants. In the initial month of a baby's life, for instance, they tend to be fed approximately eight to 12 times within a 24-hour span, dedicating as much as 20 minutes for each breastfeeding session. Consequently, during this initial month, a mother might find herself nursing for about five to eight hours per day (Dieterich et al., 2013). This practice discloses an intimate space between mothers and their children where they can bond and build together their unique relationship. Despite the uniqueness of this experience, the imperative "breast is best" that animates medical guidelines such as those from WHO and UNICEF adds indirect psychological pressure on those families who, for various reasons, cannot feed their children with their own milk and nurtures the ideology of intensive mothering that generates stress for breastfeeding mothers. As Hays (1996) shows, this ideology appoints mothers and not fathers as the automatic primary caregivers of children, creating a child-centered culture where the work and efforts put by the mothers for the survival of their children are by far more than the efforts of their partner(s). Although motherhood has been significantly influenced by increasing employment rates for women, particularly for mothers of young children, across all Western industrialized nations (O'Connor et al., 1999; Orloff, 2003), women seem still to be appointed as primary caregivers, especially if breastfeeding. Despite women taking on roles as workers, earners and sometimes primary breadwinners, they continue to be the main caregivers. Men, although traditionally primary breadwinners, have maintained a secondary role in caregiving. Many commentators note that contemporary fathers are more engaged in their children's lives compared to previous generations (O'Brien & Shemilt, 2003; E. H. Pleck & Pleck, 1997; J. H. Pleck & Masciadrelli, 2004), with notable increases in time dedicated to parenting (Gershuny, 2001; Yeung et al., 2001) and a more balanced distribution of childcare tasks (Coltrane & Adams, 2001). However, mothers still predominantly bear the responsibility for children, domestic chores and community life, a pattern that persists even where women have equal participation in paid employment (Beaujot, 2000; Coltrane, 2000; Coltrane & Adams, 2001; Doucet, 2000, 2001; Robinson & Barret, 1986; Silver, 2000).

Women are appointed as natural caregivers because often the natural way to feed their baby is through their breasts. Yet, to use Jean-Luc Nancy: "Nowhere does 'Nature' occur in a 'natural' state. Human beings have not always been there; but when they arrive the nature within them humanizes itself—that is, displaces itself in a new way" (2011, pp. 43–44).

For us, women, this naturality always comes with a double bind. As Code (2007) shows, women are often compared to nature. Their ability to procreate makes them comparable to the receptivity of nature. Today, though, we know that all that we say about nature is a construct produced by society. In fact, not all women can or want to generate life, and nature does not always look as a submissive, receptive playground where we can feel free to take as much as we can. Yet, in this *natural* setting, women are often conceived as the natural caregivers of the newborn, but at the same time, they are not the experts of what they are doing. In fact, the professionalism women gain during these hours of intense care is not left to them but to the doctor. Their intense caring activity is not acknowledged because it would be almost offensive to compare their mothering to actual work since being a mother is greatly more important than any job a person will ever accomplish. Hence, women just do what (our interpretation of) nature tells them to do, and they are not the experts of what they are doing but the mere executors.

To add to this, as Warner (2005) remarks in her book Perfect Madness: Motherhood in the Age of Anxiety, breastfeeding occurs in a vacuum where no social structure is in place to support the mother and her need to protect the child against a highly individualized society (for the author, this is true especially in the United States). Similarly, in the controversial Atlantic Monthly article titled "The Case Against Breastfeeding", journalist Rosin (2009) compared breastfeeding to "this generation's vacuum cleaner—an instrument of misery that mostly just keeps women down". Besides showing how this division of labor is such that it caters to greater freedom and power for fathers and a restricted domestic role for mothers, Rosin also emphasizes the lack of structural support to women for breastfeeding, which uncritically enshrine women's domestic roles and morally condemn those who cannot or choose not to breastfeed. In this succinct excerpt from Do Men Mother? (Doucet, 2006, p. 120), two at-home dads explain the divide between men and women created by breastfeeding with these words:

> A few fathers reiterate these sentiments, but most suggest an embodied basis for the differences between mothers and fathers. Alistair, who stayed home for over a year with his first infant daughter, is aware of the physical connections associated with pregnancy, birth, and breastfeeding, and also of women's overall emotional involvement, especially with young children: "I think you are so physically involved as a mother, from the beginning. Nine months of pregnancy—such a commitment—and then into the breastfeeding. And then normally mothers are much more involved with taking care of very small babies. There is a tremendous bond right there. Even when I was taking care of Georgia at home, I didn't have the same physical bond as Claire did with this baby. I think women are more sensitive and more inclined to be emotionally involved". Gary, a carpenter and stay-at-home father of three boys, succinctly captures many of the fathers' views on this matter when he speaks about how his wife, Kathy, relates to the kids: "Well, like I said, men do nurture. We do give them a hug, tell them it's okay, sit them on our knee. But I just find with the mother they do it more or longer. They give a tighter hug".

At the moment, since WHO recognized the crucial role of breastfeeding for the well-being of the baby, more breastfeeding plans are in place to support breastfeeding families.[1] These plans, though, hardly consider breastfeeding as a human experience pertaining to women and all the network of people involved in their intimate lives. The plans appear as a utilitarian list of pros and cons created to persuade women to choose this path rather than others. In this list, personal values, emotions and the physical and psychological limitations experienced by the mothers and their intimate network seem to be absent.

II. Breastfeeding Is a Lived Experience

The MIYCN plan outlines six WHO global nutrition targets to be accomplished by the year 2025, one of which is increasing exclusive breastfeeding among infants younger than six months to 50%. Breastfeeding is unanimously considered the healthy choice to guarantee the development of the baby and increase the chances of a fast recovery for the mother.

While honorable, this plan does not seem to treat breastfeeding as a very personal lived experience as it leaves out the emotional charge involved in the decision.

From what we know in the literature, women are aware of what is more useful for them, but they have to make the best choices for themselves and their babies given the situation in which they are living (Heidari et al., 2017). One out of two women who desire to breastfeed their babies for at least two months stops after six weeks because they find it challenging to continue (DiGirolamo et al., 2008; Mozingo et al., 2000). If you consider the brevity of maternal leave and the intense amount of work required to keep the milk going without health concerns for mothers and their babies, then it is easy to guess at least one of the reasons why this task cannot be reached. Concerns about maternal or child health (infant nutrition, maternal illness or the need for medicine for the mother and infant illness), processes associated with breastfeeding (lactation and milk-pumping problems), lack of professional support and lack of positive influence from the partner(s) are some of the reasons behind an early stop of breastfeeding. Not to mention the almost nonexistent professional and scientific concern of the maternal well-being during the fourth trimester; this time holds the highest health risk potential for the mother to the extent that (Choi et al., 2022; Benson & Wolf, 2012) in the United States 84% of preventable maternal deaths are in this fourth trimester (CDC, 2013 report). The body is trying to get to its pre-pregnant state; the hormonal fluctuation, the swelling, the fatigue and the lower defenses of the immune system can make this time very delicate and yet still very neglected. Moreover, maternal suicide is also a leading cause of maternal mortality during this fourth trimester, with rates of suicide peaking in the postpartum period (Staneva et al., 2017; McNamara et al., 2019; Gavin et al., 2011). Though some issues occurring in the fourth trimester are pretty common—among which heavy vaginal bleeding; urinary incontinence; fecal incontinence; hemorrhoids; constipation; fractured tailbone; calf pain (deep vein thrombosis); abdominal pain from C-section incision; first-, second-, third- and fourth-degree tears from vaginal delivery; pelvic thrombosis; pulmonary embolism; hematoma in the groin and abdomen; anal fissures; fistula; separation of the symphysis pubis; and infections of the uterus, urinary tract, perineum and cervix (Benson & Wolf, 2012)—no particular care is offered to her except for the mandatory OB/GYN six-week appointment, which is a quite general checkup. To heal—or to even understand that there's something to heal from—the busy mother in distress has to hunt for information on the web and more often educate herself through phone applications (which opens another Pandora's box that I addressed in Ferrarello, 2024).

If none of these experiential factors are duly understood, it seems that breastfeeding, although desirable, will remain a difficult task to accomplish. This practice will remain a golden rule not achievable for many as far as it keeps being conceived not as a complex personal experience but as a set of guidelines bestowed upon women for their well-being and the well-being of their children, especially when these guidelines will continue to exclude them—the true protagonists of this experience—from the expertise that they actually gain from it.

III. The Sinful Breasts

In terms of exclusivity, not much has seemingly changed since the seventeenth century onward. For example, during the seventeenth century in American colonies, the physician James Nelson advised women to breastfeed until their babies were four months old or their men decided so (Treckel, 1989, p. 36). According to the available sources, men were the principal responsible for the decision to put their children with wet nurses or stop breastfeeding. Independent of the desire or will of the mothers to breastfeed their babies, it was often men's desire to resume sexual activities to decide the length of breastfeeding (Koehler, 1980). It was a belief that menstrual blood and milk were the same substance but in a different state; resuming sexual activities would have turned the milk into blood, hence damaging the growth of the baby. That is why women were strongly encouraged to not even have sexual thoughts while breastfeeding (Carter, 1995). Resuming sexual activity would have contaminated infants' milk. On the other hand, women who chose not to breastfeed to please their husbands' (or their own) sexual desire were accordingly considered sinful and Eve-like by puritan reformers in America and England in the seventeenth century.

Even more startling is to read that until the late 1600s all authorities around infants and their development believed that it was detrimental for the development of the baby to latch the baby at birth (Sharp, 1671; Maubray, 1724); rather, they were fed with sweetened wine or "the breast of some other clean and sound woman" (Maubray, 1724). Because the colostrum was considered poisonous, breastfeeding was recommended only after the colostrum left the breast of the mother—the method to "cleanse" the woman from her colostrum was made possible by the aid of puppies' and/or midwives' suckle (Fox, 1966). Hence, babies—the wealthy ones were sent to wet nursing—and women, poor and wealthy ones, died from simple mastitis (because of the milk stagnating in the breast) and/or breast infections due to poor hygiene.

Despite the fact that we dispose of better medical knowledge, today, like yesterday, women's choice about how and when to feed their infants is strongly based on guidelines that treat breastfeeding more as a medical practice rather than as a very personal experience. Those who are in fact involved in this practice are excluded from the expertise they gain from it and cut off from their very instincts. According to the study conducted by Heidari et al. (2017), empowerment in breastfeeding can be achieved through acquiring personal understanding of one's own skills, along with confidence in the quality and quantity of the mother's milk. Successfully addressing breastfeeding challenges also contributes to stable empowerment in breastfeeding. Additionally, feeling the value of breastfeeding enhances empowerment, and receiving comprehensive support for breastfeeding further facilitates ongoing empowerment.

IV.   Disembodiment and Loss of Agency

Understanding breastfeeding as a way of life helps illuminate the myriad of things a new mother must learn as she enters this new territory. Even for a second- or third-time mother, breastfeeding is always a new learning curve because each baby is different. This contact always brings new aspects to learn about herself and the child, unfolding a new, shared world from their connection. For this unfolding to occur, it is essential for the woman to feel ownership of her body and a sense of agency through it.

Breastfeeding might alter the way a woman conducts her life in many ways. She might feel disembodied given the time she needs to spend on the couch breastfeeding (or pumping for) her child (Williams, 2019). Everything might remain the same—same abode, same friends, same partner(s)—but her world has completely changed. Metaphorically speaking, the mother-baby bond is such that the skin of the woman's body becomes, so to speak, tighter. There is still space for both, but with more pressure "to be" because they both want to be. For example, one wants to eat, the other one wants to take a walk; one wants to cuddle, the other one wants to sleep. This one body has to find a way to make both organisms happy. In this challenge, the pressure to succeed in coming to being becomes higher and higher. Moreover, under this pressure, it also happens that the mother no longer has a body to interact with others. Despite the crucial importance that her body holds for the survival of the baby, it might very well be that the only body perceived is the infant's because this body is literally on her most of the day. Even the closest people around her might be able to see only the infant's body. Dressing her own body might feel awkward at times because it becomes functional to spend the day with the baby without the time to feel herself in her own clothes. Hence, a vicious circle of missing each other's bodies takes place. Husbands miss their wives (and vice versa), older children miss their mamas (and vice versa) and so on.

Moreover, she might perceive that her old (embodied) self is swallowed by the sacred halo of nature operating through her body (Farhadi, 2020). For believers, breastfeeding might even extend its implications on the sense of agency and embodiment that the breastfeeding mother perceives over her purpose in life (Laroia & Sharma, 2006; Shaikh & Ahmed, 2006). The woman is expected to embody a certain sacred model that does not necessarily coincide with her authentic self.

Because of the sacredness that surrounds this experience, any ambiguous feeling about her recent metamorphosis will be brushed off by saying that this is a blessing one should be grateful for. This body is apparently sacred as it generates life and produces a healing juice that will keep her baby alive. Nevertheless, from this space of sacredness, it is very difficult to function for the woman as she did before; activities as simple as exercising, experiencing sexual pleasure, and eating and drinking favorite foods might now be very difficult to perform. No particular medical and/or psychological guidance is offered. Even drinking water becomes a new experience for the mother, as she will feel an intense thirst she rarely felt before. She will need to explain to those around her how important it is to have a glass of water nearby, especially when she is alone breastfeeding the baby on the couch or at night in her room.

The main imperative ruling over her body is the production of milk, because this is what will keep her baby alive. Even if in doing so she is complying with the natural teleology of her body, this demand might still feel unknown and unusual to her old sense of identity. If a woman lacks the physical or emotional energy to connect with her new body and nurture her child, she must learn how to cope with the overwhelming amount of warnings about the dangers associated with formula feeding—all the while being sleep-deprived and fatigued. The little creature might get sick, suffer from brain deficit, type 2 diabetes or even die from simple infections because their immune system will be low without breast milk—at least, so they are told (Stuebe, 2009; Krol & Grossmann, 2018). If we allow this imperative to dominate our lives, the process of self-discovery and learning in this new world with the baby becomes increasingly difficult. When milk production becomes an obsession for the new mother, her connection with her body suffers. Reduced to a mere technique, breastfeeding ceases to be about bonding and getting to know each other; it becomes mainly about how much milk this now alienated body can produce.

Avishai (2007) acknowledges how, for some women, breastfeeding often becomes a completely disembodied project that does not provide particular pleasure to the woman. Taking classes, having home visits to learn how to lactate and being taught at the hospital how to connect effectively with the baby transform the breastfeeding experience into an intellectual activity where the goal is to fulfill the duty. That is, to prove to oneself that they can nurse and they can provide for the well-being of their own child. The body becomes a machine set in motion to achieve a very specific goal. Any failure is to be condemned with shame. On the other hand, in this same study, Avishai shows how women, in particular black women, regain agency over their bodies by rejecting medical advice about breastfeeding or simply taking pleasure in what they do when they are doing it. "The doctors said that breastmilk was the best, but I told them I didn't want to. They tried to talk me into it, but they couldn't", one interviewee said (2007, p. 138). As Campbell and Meynell (2009) noticed, when the practice of breastfeeding is not seen as an embodied activity, women are expropriated of their own bodies and forced into an intellectual exercise where what counts is the utilitarian goal to fulfill the duty. When breastfeeding is embraced as a conscious choice, free from technicalities and societal pressure (such as returning to work earlier than one is ready for), it can significantly enhance one's life. Despite the challenges that many first-time mothers are unaware of, breastfeeding can bring immense pleasure and rewards. Breastfeeding as a way of life is a comprehensive approach that celebrates the profound connection between mother and baby, recognizing its significance beyond mere nutrition. It encompasses emotional bonding, physical health, mutual growth, resilience in facing challenges, seamless integration into daily life and awareness of cultural and social dimensions. By embracing breastfeeding in this holistic manner, we honor the deep and lasting impact it has on both mother and child, fostering a nurturing environment that supports their journey together.

V. New Life-Worlds

While deciding to breastfeed, the usual social and emotional barriers of an average life remain: struggles at work, short maternity leave, sickness, unstable partnerships and households, daily expenses, hormonal upheaval and similar. From her usual life-world, at least three new life-worlds will be generated: her new one, the shared world with her child, and the life-world of her child.

Here is the revised version:

Life-world is a phenomenological concept, typically Husserlian (1936), that refers to the way in which we live in the world and process meaning through and with it. We might experience life under the wrong assumption that what we see in front of us is the same for everyone, but this would limit our ability to interact in society with each other. Clearly, for an infant, her mother is their whole world, while the mother comes from a life-world that is much wider and populated by her family, friends, job, places she likes to go. Through breastfeeding the mother generates a meaningful contact with the new life-world of the baby or better she expands the connection that was previously created in the belly toward a safe and reassuring direction. In this extremely delicate process it might happen that, so to speak, not enough nutrients are going to feed the variety of the three worlds. The woman would not only need special multivitamins to sustain her physical body, but also a metaphorical set of multivitamins to sustain the germination of these life-worlds. The life-world she shared with her friends, colleagues, family, husband has deeply changed and in some cases it is no longer there. The new shared world she is sharing with her baby stems from her own life-world, mostly represented by the plasticity of her own body, passions, and skills belonging to herself. Yet, different from any other shared-world encounters where everyone brings its own life-world in the constitution of a shared one, in the encounter with a baby's life-world there is a sort of a blank slate where everything is amazement and novelty. When breastfeeding mother and baby explore the mother's body as a means to mirror the future exploration of the baby's body and enhance his/her skills (more on this in chapters 4 and 6); that helps create those meanings from which the world around starts making sense.

If in this process the mother is left alone, either out of good intentions to give her some privacy or for lack of genuine care, problems might arise. In fact, if she finds herself isolated (Dominus, 2023) while in the process of creating a new shared world, her own life-world might collapse on the life-world of her child. That is why encouraging isolation and/or shaming her attempts to reconnect with her usual life might be very damaging in this delicate phase.

V.1   Brexting: Shame on You!

One example of shaming against women is related to their use of mobile phones. As Dominus (2023) rightly points out, Western society seems to have a high tolerance for women's pain. The model of natural, intensive, self-sacrificing and isolated motherhood seems to be taken for granted in our society. Women are expected to ensure their baby's thriving and survival, or else they risk losing the title of being "natural" caregivers. It is considered unnatural for a mother to be incapable of taking care of her children; if she fails to do so, she is seen as going against nature. Yet it is not against nature to shame them when trying to connect to the world. For example, brexting (texting while breastfeeding), experts say, undermines the bonding process between mothers and their children. Distracted mothers might miss important bodily messages from their children if they use their phones[2]:

> "You assist them latching on and you can see the phone buzzing, they're getting an alert or something, and you see their eyes move down and look at it," says Bretscher. "Sometimes they will actually answer that right then and we go, 'well let's work on this now'".

It is clear why experts condemn messaging while breastfeeding; yet it is likewise clear the need for mothers to break isolation from the outside world. The phone represents a multidimensional door that not only helps the mother to remain awake during night feeding, but it also bridges the woman to her old life-world, where her friends, family and job are still unchanged and maybe waiting for her return. It represents a hope to still have a place in her life-world and the society to which she felt connected. It is true that a behavior such as brexting might slow down the constitution of the shared life-world with her child because she might miss important cues, but it should be left to the mother to decide when and how to bond with her child.

Moreover, another example of isolation for mothers is the answer received when breastfeeding in public spaces. Despite a state law in the United States giving mothers the right to breastfeed in public, this practice has been often seen as socially reprehensible. In the United States in 2007, a nursing mother was asked to cover herself or leave the restaurant. The Applebee's chain supported the decision of the waiter, who asked the woman to leave. Similarly, Facebook in 2009 removed photos of breastfeeding mothers because they retained showing these photos violated the decency standards of the website. Breastfeeding has been in some way perceived as indecent and accordingly implicitly invited women to pursue this practice in their homes.

If breastfeeding is considered indecent and shameful because it exposes the body of the woman, then the woman is implicitly asked to remain isolated for a great part of her days. Practically, this would translate into having to say no to activities as simple as meals with friends, breakfasts in nice cafés or gatherings with family because it is too scandalous for her to feed her babies in these venues. The woman who might already perceive discomfort and shame toward a body that no longer seems to belong to her might feel even worse if society tells her to feel ashamed of herself while practicing what is presented as a vital activity for the present and future wealth of her child.

V.2   The Price of Isolation

This picture can help us give a more personable framework where to locate WHO/UNICEF initiatives, such as the Baby-Friendly Hospital Initiative (BFHI). This is a program developed by the World Health Organization (WHO) and the United Nations Children's Fund (UNICEF) that has been devised to promote breastfeeding in hospitals and birthing facilities worldwide. The program was launched in 1991 in order to increase breastfeeding initiation, duration and exclusivity. All nurses—whether they work in maternity care or another nursing specialty in a hospital, ambulatory or community setting—are asked to play a crucial role in promoting societal health through their support of long-term breastfeeding as recommended by the WHO and UNICEF. Yet, as mentioned earlier, these initiatives do not consider breastfeeding as a lived experience but as a medical practice. It is in one of those hospitals in Rome that, in the fall of 2023, a mother accidentally smothered her baby while breastfeeding.[3] Even though she repeatedly asked to opt out of the room-in service (where they let the baby stay with the woman without her person of support) because she was extremely tired from the delivery, the nurses told her that it would have been good for her and her baby to bond together in the room even if she was tired. Unfortunately, the woman fell asleep while breastfeeding and accidentally killed her newborn baby. She woke up to an empty crib. After this event, a wave of women shared their stories in solidarity with hers, all of which had in common the same trait—the choice of breastfeeding was not left to them. Their personal experience and preference were not heard. There was always someone else who knew better what was good for them and their children. In this case, as in many others, the room-in option to favor breastfeeding was an imposition from above that left the woman alone with a high-responsibility task after the most exhausting hours of their lives.

While I believe that WHO and UNICEF strive to provide better care for all and encourage breastfeeding because it actually helps babies to thrive, I strongly insist on the importance of seeing breastfeeding as a very complex and high-pressure experience that does not involve only the woman but all the network of people around her. As rightly Guttman and Zimmerman (2000) pointed out, women are well aware of the health advantages of breast milk. They do not need to be educated by the massive public health campaigns that advocate for it from above (Kukla, 2005); if they choose not to breastfeed, they do so because of concrete social impediments such as the social isolation earlier described, inadequate maternal leaves, a lack of safe space to breastfeed in (both at home and at work), disapproval of breastfeeding by other family members and unhelpful advice from medical professionals and discomfort with breastfeeding in public (Boyer 430). Women do not stop breastfeeding because they lack education or concern about the goodness of their babies (Carter 206). The reasons women fail to breastfeed are not linked to irrationality or lack of understanding on the part of mothers about the benefit of breastfeeding.

VI. A Conclusion: Choosing to Be the Primary Caregiver

I would like to discuss what De Beauvoir (1989) describes as the tyranny of the baby. For some women, the infant

> seems to be sucking out her strength, her life, her happiness. It inflicts a harsh slavery upon her and it is no longer a part of her: it seems a tyrant; she feels hostile to this little stranger, this individual who menaces her flesh, her freedom, her whole ego.
>
> *(1989, p. 508)*

At times, the bonding relationship between infant and mother leads to a restriction of the agency of the mother and the freedom of her actual movements, but that does not necessarily be so. As a society, we can grow to offer more support and more chances of happiness for those women who decide to become mothers, also the breastfeeding ones. Unhappy mothers make unhappy children, and these children will grow as unhappy adults in the society.

> According to Shulz . . . the basic questions about human capital are: Who will bear the costs? Who will reap the benefits? The answer to the first question is families, and mothers in particular. The answer to the second question is everyone. The entire society benefits from well raised children, without sharing more than a fraction of the costs of producing them. And that free ride on female labor is enforced by every major institution, starting with the workplace.
>
> *(Crittenden, 2001, p. 86)*

It is for the good of everyone to pay attention to the decency of the quality of life of women, being aware of the life-altering and life-threatening events that birth represents and building around that an intelligent network in support of her agency, body in continuity with her life-world.

Similarly to de Beauvoir, Kukla writes that breastfeeding conflicts with women's autonomy. She asserts that

> A woman who feels that she cannot leave her infant, or even reasonably deny her infant any form of access to her body, cannot do the concrete things that normal humans need to do in order to have a meaningful, distinct identity that is comprehensible to themselves and others.
>
> *(2005, p. 178)*

This occurs if the woman holds both a maternalist and a medical model of breastfeeding (Blum, 2000). This latter is based on a utilitarian list of pros and cons on the basis of which doctors almost determine the future well-being of that person for the rest of their life (if duly breastfed, the baby will have a better immune system, brain development, fewer allergies etc.). The former instead assumes that women treasure breastfeeding because it creates a unique bond between mothers and their children. This assumption implies that all mothers are suited to be the primary caregiver and find that close physical contact fulfilling.

Both assumptions are clearly biased. A utilitarian list of pros and cons can provide reasons, but it cannot embody the experience of breastfeeding and motivate a mother to lose her agency in it. Not all mothers are suited for this experience as primary caregivers; this does not make them less of a mother or unnatural human beings. As Wall shows, both models make the mother a subject invisible in her needs and wants (Wall, 2001, p. 604). A significant recovery of autonomy and connection to their usual life-world with its meaning, functioning and expectations would be possible if both partners were given the choice to be the primary caregivers or not. Mothering can be pleasurable without damaging the identity and autonomy of the woman irreversibly.

Earle (2002) found that some mothers turn to formula feeding in an effort to re-establish their identities prior to motherhood as separate individuals. As Blum (2000) remarks, in breastfeeding, the gender inequality becomes immediately apparent because the main job of sustaining a baby's life is given to the woman. The partner is not asked what role they will play in that basic survival if not for going to work and gaining the bacon to sustain the family. This feeds paradoxes and reasons for resentments that can undermine the sense of intimacy in the couple and the happiness of the future family. But if dutifully explored, assigning roles can open to new possibilities in gender equality. For this reason, we need to keep in mind that it is up to the parents to ultimately choose how to sustain the lives of their children. Campaigns that bomb with messages in one direction or another (breastfeeding or formula) are both unfair for the agency of a couple—in particular the mother—who is getting ready to sustain the survival of her little baby.

Notes

1 See https://www.who.int/health-topics/breastfeeding#tab=tab_1
2 https://www.kpcc.org/2015-09-24/brexting-impacts-baby-bonding-during-breastfeeding
3 See https://tg24.sky.it/cronaca/2023/01/24/mamma-bimbo-morto-ospedale

References

Avishai, O. (2007). Managing the lactating body: The breast-feeding project and privileged motherhood. *Qualitative Sociology, 30*, 135–152.
Beaujot, R. (2000). *Earning and caring in Canadian families*. Broadview Press.
Beauvoir, S. (1989). *The second sex*. Random House of Canada.
Benson, J., & Wolf, A. (2012). Where did I go. In S. Lintott & M. Sander-Staudt (Eds.), *Philosophical inquiries into pregnancy, childbirth, and mothering: Maternal subjects* (pp. 34–49). Routledge.
Blum, L. (2000). *At the breast: Ideologies of breastfeeding and motherhood in the contemporary United States*. Beacon Press.
Campbell, S., & Meynell, L. (2009). *Embodiment and agency*. Penn State Press.
Carter, P. (1995). *Feminism, breasts and breastfeeding*. St. Martin's Press.
CDC. (2013). https://www.cdc.gov/media/releases/2022/p0919-pregnancy-related-deaths.html
Choi, E., Kazzi, B., Varma, B., Ortengren, A. R., Minhas, A. S., Vaught, A. J., Bennett, W. L., Lewey, J., & Michos, E. D. (2022). The fourth trimester: A time for enhancing transitions in cardiovascular care. *Current Cardiovascular Risk Reports, 16*(12), 219–229.
Code, L. (2007). *Ecological thinking: The politics of epistemic location*. Oxford University Press.

Coltrane, S. (2000). Research on household labor: Modeling and measuring the social embeddedness of routine family work. *Journal of Marriage and the Family*, *62*(November), 1208–1233.

Coltrane, S., & Adams, M. (2001). Men's family work: Child-centered fathering and the sharing of domestic labor. In N. L. Marshall (Ed.), *Working families: The transformation of the American home* (pp. 72–102). University of California Press.

Crittenden, A. (2001). *The price of motherhood: Why the most important job in the world is still the least valued*. Metropolitan Books.

Dieterich, C. M., Felice, J. P., O'Sullivan, E., & Rasmussen, K. M. (2013). Breastfeeding and health outcomes for the mother-infant dyad. *Pediatric Clinics of North America*, *60*(1), 31–48.

DiGirolamo, A., Grummer-Strawn, L., & Fein, S. (2008). Infant feeding practices study II: Study methods. *Pediatrics*, *122*(2), 28–35.

Dominus, S. (2023). *The Sunday read: 'Women have been misled about menopause'*. https://www.nytimes.com/2023/02/12/podcasts/the-daily/menopause-treatment-hormone-therapy.html

Doucet, A. (2000). 'There's a huge difference between me as a male carer and women': Gender, domestic responsibility, and the community as an institutional arena. *Community Work and Family*, *3*(2), 163–184.

Doucet, A. (2001). Can boys grow into mothers? Maternal thinking and fathers' reflections. In A. O'Reilly (Ed.), *Mothers and sons: Feminism, masculinity and the struggle to raise our sons* (pp. 163–82). Routledge.

Doucet, A. (2006). *Do men mother?* University of Toronto Press.

Earle, S. (2002). Factors affecting the initiation of breastfeeding: Implications for breastfeeding promotion. *Health Promotion International*, *17*(3), 205–214.

Farhadi, R. (2020). Spiritual aspects of breastfeeding: A narrative review. *Journal of Pediatrics Review*, *8*(4), 229–236.

Ferrarello, S. (2024). Technology, intimacy and motherhood. In *New Techno Humanities*. ISSN 2664–3294. https://doi.org/10.1016/j.techum.2024.05.001

Fox, C. (1966). *Pregnancy, childbirth and early infancy in Anglo-American culture, 1675–1830* [Unpublished PhD dissertation, University of Pennsylvania].

Gavin, A. R., Tabb, K. M., Melville, J. L., Guo, Y., & Katon, W. (2011). Prevalence and correlates of suicidal ideation during pregnancy. *Archives of Women's Mental Health*, *14*(3), 239–246.

Gershuny, J. I. (2001). *Changing times*. Oxford University Press.

Guttman, N., & Zimmerman, D. R. (2000). Low-income mothers' views on breastfeeding. *Social Science & Medicine*, *50*(10), 1457–1473.

Hays, S. (1996). *The cultural contradictions of motherhood*. Yale University Press.

Heidari, Z., Kohan, S., & Keshvari, M. (2017). Empowerment in breastfeeding as viewed by women: A qualitative study. *Journal of Education and Health Promotion*, *6*, 33.

Koehler, L. (1980). *The search for power: Weaker sex in seventeenth century New England*. University of Illinois Press.

Krol, K. M., & Grossmann, T. (2018). Psychological effects of breastfeeding on children and mothers. Psychologische Effekte des Stillens auf Kinder und Mütter. *Bundesgesundheitsblatt, Gesundheitsforschung, Gesundheitsschutz*, *61*(8), 977–985.

Kukla, R. (2005). *Mass hysteria: Medicine, culture, and mothers' bodies*. Rowman & Littlefield.

Laroia, N., & Sharma, D. (2006). The religious and cultural bases for breastfeeding practices among the Hindus. *Breastfeeding Medicine: The Official Journal of the Academy of Breastfeeding Medicine*, *1*(2), 94–98.

Maubray, J. (1724). *The female physician John Maubray, the female physician, containing all the diseases incident to that sex, in virgins, wives, and widows; together with their causes and symptoms.* London Press.

McFadden, A., Siebelt, L., Marshall, J. L., Gavine, A., Girard, L. C., Symon, A., & MacGillivray, S. (2019). Counselling interventions to enable women to initiate and continue breastfeeding: A systematic review and meta-analysis. *International Breastfeeding Journal, 14,* 42.

McNamara, J., Townsend, M. L., & Herbert, J. S. (2019). A systemic review of maternal wellbeing and its relationship with maternal fetal attachment and early postpartum bonding. *PLoS One, 14*(7).

Mozingo, J. N., Davis, M. W., Droppleman, P. G., & Merideth, A. (2000). "It wasn't working." Women's experiences with short-term breastfeeding. *MCN: The American Journal of Maternal Child Nursing, 25*(3), 120–126.

Nancy, J.-L. (2011). *Sexistence* (S. Miller, Trans.). Fordham University Press.

O'Brien, M., & Shemilt, I. (2003). *Working fathers: Earning and caring.* Equal Opportunities Commission.

O'Connor, J. S., Orloff, A. S., & Shaver, S. (1999). *States, markets, families: Gender, liberalism, and social policy in Australia, Canada, Great Britain, and the United States.* Cambridge University Press.

Orloff, A. (2003). al "Market not States". Review 58(3):303-2 the U.S. pp. 217–245. In L. A. Haney & L. Polland (Eds.), *Families of a new world: Gender, context.* Routledge.

Pleck, E. H., & Pleck, J. H. (1997). Fatherhood ideals in the United States: Historical dimensions. In M. E. Lamb (Ed.), *The role of the father in child development.* Wiley.

Pleck, J. H., & Masciadrelli, B. P. (2004). Parental involvement: Levels, sources and consequences. In M. E. Lamb (Ed.), *The role of the father in child development* (4th ed., pp. 222–271). Wiley.

Robinson, B. E., & Barret, R. L. (1986). *The developing father: Emerging roles in contemporary society.* Guilford.

Rosin, H. (2009). The case against breastfeeding. *The Atlantic, 4.* https://www.theatlantic.com/magazine/archive/2009/04/the-case-against-breast-feeding/307311/

Shaikh, U., & Ahmed, O. (2006). Islam and infant feeding. *Breastfeeding Medicine: The Official Journal of the Academy of Breastfeeding Medicine, 1*(3), 164–167.

Sharp, J. (1671). *The midwives book: On the whole ART of midwifery discovered. Directing childbearing women how to behave themselves.* Printed for S. Miller.

Silver, C. (2000). *Being there: The time dual-earner couples spend with their children.* Statistics Canada.

Staneva, A. A., Bogossian, F., Morawska, A., & Wittkowski, A. (2017). "I just feel like I am broken. I am the worst pregnant woman ever": A qualitative exploration of the "at odds" experience of women's antenatal distress. *Health Care for Women International, 38*(6), 658–686.

Stuebe, A. (2009). The risks of not breastfeeding for mothers and infants. *Reviews in Obstetrics & Gynecology, 2*(4), 222–231.

Treckel, P. (1989). Breastfeeding and maternal sexuality in colonial America. *The Journal of Interdisciplinary History,* 25–51.

Wall, G. (2001). Moral constructions of motherhood in breastfeeding discourse. *Gender and Society, 15*(4), 592–610.

Warner, J. (2005). *Perfect madness: Motherhood in the age of anxiety.* Riverhead.

Williams, H. R. (2019). "Effective disembodiment:" Female patienthood and reproductive health in Elisa Albert's *after birth* and Pamela Erens's *eleven hours. Contemporary Women's Writing, 13*(1), 34–52.

Yeung, W. J., Sandberg, J. F., Davis-Kean, P. E., & Hofferth, S. L. (2001). Children's time with fathers in intact families. *Journal of Marriage and the Family, 63*(1), 1360154.

4

THE CLASH OF VOLITIONS

Do I Want What My Baby Wants?

I. Introduction

"If you are not a mother, you cannot understand". I have always found this expression somewhat offensive and dismissive. A variation of this saying that my mother often used to conclude our arguments was: "When you become a mother, you will understand why I do what I do". Having had my first child later in life, these sayings created a longstanding wall between me and all the women who subscribed to them. We probably both felt isolated on our respective sides of this wall. What is so difficult to verbalize, and I see with a little more clarity today, is that early motherhood confronts us with the limits of our volitions and the fragility of our willpower. This fragility endangers the sense of control we can exert on who we are and who we want to become. Similar to the other chapters of the book, in this, too, I will put in every effort to find words to explain this experience and reduce the thickness of the wall that separates us.

Let's start with a simple example: a mother's body might need a shower and some rest, while the baby's body might require care and nourishment. What was once a personal conflict of desires and choices before pregnancy becomes, in motherhood, a clash of volitions that touches the deepest roots of a woman's being. This conflict occurs multiple times a day and even more frequently over the course of a week, to the point where the mother is no longer aware of what she needs or is unable to attend to her own basic needs.

Having children confronts women with a bodily logic that is seldom experienced before motherhood and can seem almost illogical. During pregnancy, a woman finds herself hosting another being within her body and nurturing this being through her own physical resources. This places her in the unique situation

DOI: 10.4324/9781003490937-4

of being both herself and another at the same time. Moreover, after pregnancy, another counterintuitive process begins, which I would call symbiotic individuation. The woman continues to be both herself and another at the same time. The newborn depends entirely on her—especially if she chooses to be the primary caregiver—while she simultaneously prepares the child to venture out into the world and find independence. Both mother and child strive for individuation while living in a symbiotic relationship. In fact, the motivational force driving the woman's organic body operates in a counterintuitive manner. The concept of exterogestation (Montagu, 1961) suggests that a mother's well-being aligns with the preservation of the growing life, despite her immediate personal needs potentially being directed elsewhere. For the nine months following delivery, individuation occurs through this symbiotic connection, where volitions and their fulfillment take unpredictable paths.

Accordingly, the transition to motherhood presents women with psychological and practical challenges that make their adjustment to their new identity cumbersome and epistemologically complex to understand (Hine et al., 2019; Laney et al., 2015). Different motivational undercurrents shape this lived experience, and these currents do not always align with one another. In this chapter, I will focus on the interaction between time, will and motivation to illuminate one of the many motivational currents driving this challenging transition toward individuation.

I believe that if this transition is not achieved, it may result in a performative use of gender (Butler, 1988) and, consequently, a loss of individuation for the mother, the child or both. If neither the baby nor the mother finds a way to individuate within the new forms their bodies take, they risk maintaining their symbiotic relationship in a way that favors either the mother or the child. This can lead to performing their roles according to societal scripts rather than achieving true individuation.

Therefore, in this chapter, I will first discuss the type of logic that might apply to the experience of pregnancy. I will then use Husserl's theory of motivation to examine how our motivation interacts with the will and the concept of time.

II. The Logic of Embodied Interrelation

The experience of pregnancy and early motherhood is so complex that even the structure of our language fails us, leaving us unable to articulate its intricacies. How do we grasp the ontological complexity of being oneself and yet not entirely oneself at the same time? How do we explain the challenge of being oneself and another simultaneously within the same body? How can we conceive of the transition from being two in one to becoming a single entity again? Most importantly, what impact do these questions have on a woman's psychological sense of self and well-being? Furthermore, how does an unsuccessful transition affect a child's development?

During this unique stage of life, a woman must stretch her logic to perceive herself as at least three different beings: the person she has always known, the new person taking on the role of mother and the being growing inside her. Contrary to Aristotle's logic, which posits that A cannot be both A and non-A at the same time, in pregnancy, a woman is and is not herself simultaneously within the same body. As Bornemark writes:

> In our everyday life it is mostly unproblematic to accept that the chair is a chair and the table is a table. I am I, and you are you. The words fit the experience and are useful. But there are occasions when this is no longer the case; when every word seems to be too strong and say too much. Pregnancy is one of those occasions. Something is going on in pregnancy that does not fit our everyday language. Basic concepts, such as "one" and "two", "self" and "other", "me" and "you", are no longer simple, but complicated and misleading.
>
> *(Bornemark, 2023, p. 128)*

In this unique transitional phase, a woman finds herself in a psychic border space where co-emergence and separation in jointness are possible (Ettinger, 2006a, 2006b). During pregnancy, the woman prepares to become someone she is not yet—a mother—in virtue of nurturing a being made of her own flesh, but which will ultimately become separate from her. As two personal accounts of this experience report:

> The child that I carry for nine months can be defined neither as me or as not-me.
>
> *(cited in Rich, 1977, p. 64)*

> Looking back . . . I find it the most typical of the pregnant state of mind-rambling, torn between the external and the internal.
>
> *(cited in Lewis, 1951, p. 131)*

This transition makes it challenging to distinguish between inside and outside, one and two, me and you. Women report a state of confusion during this period (Razurel et al., 2011), necessitating adaptation and transformation on multiple levels—physical, cultural and social. In this context, Bornemark suggests integrating Aristotle's logic with that of Nicholas of Cusa to foster a more comprehensive understanding of the logic underlying the transition from pregnancy to motherhood. Nicholas of Cusa himself believed that Aristotle's logic should not be excluded but rather integrated into a broader framework capable of embracing the concrete ontological mystery of the unknown, which simultaneously defines our existence. This is a logic capable of transcending its own concrete limits (Ziebart, 2013, pp. 64–72). In the words of Nicholas of Cusa:

> Because other is other than something, it lacks that which it is other. But because Not-other [non-aliud] is not other than anything, it does not lack anything, nor can anything exist outside of it. Hence, without Not-other [non-aliud] no thing can be spoken of or thought of.
>
> *(Cusa,* On Not-other, *6:20)*

According to Nicholas of Cusa, the power of non-aliud, the "not other" from what is to be, resides precisely in this relational and existential essence; the "not other" is what differs from us yet coexists with us in order to be. This embodied relationality makes our volitions more challenging to achieve. The "not other" than anything represents the interconnectedness of all things. What comes into being exists precisely in this relational coincidentia oppositorum (coincidence of opposites). The multifaceted nature of our existence grows through the recognition of being distinct from the "not other". Existence is because of this non-aliud, and is this non-aliud, in relation to which we gradually conquer more terrain, much like a polygon inscribed in a circle—using Nicholas of Cusa's famous imagery.

In a woman's life, the logic governing the motivational force behind the transition to a new identity appears to be guided by this absolute non-aliud, which, like the mystery of life, grows within her womb. We will describe later how this non-aliud intertwines with the motivational force guiding a woman's transition to motherhood.

III. Feeling at Home in the Symbiotic Individuation: Motivations

Husserl's philosophical interpretation of nature, free from social constructs and human projections, can assist us in grasping the unique logic of pregnancy and motherhood. Husserl views nature as a fundamental unity that embodies an ontological order (Hua XXXVII, 103) and a universal interconnectedness that transcends intellectual comprehension, being accessible only through the realm of emotions (Gemüt). He defines the natural as that which intuitively feels correct without requiring additional justification—a guiding principle that governs all phenomena.

Husserl refers to the natural realm of basic emotions (instincts, impulses and emotions) as the lower spirit or mind, depending on the translation of the German word "Geist" that we choose to adopt (Hua 37, 107). This lower aspect is not an ego but rather nature in its purest form, embodying the primal and authentic flow of existence. At this level, we engage with the essence of nature itself, as we are an integral part of nature.

On this level, a layer of primal emotions and instincts continually sediment in habits that will form our personality on a more passive level, referred to by Husserl as the subpersonal spirit (Hua XXXIX, 422, 483). This is the stage from which motivations, interests and volitions emerge; here, our subjectivity has not yet fully awakened, but our inherent instinctual ways of reacting and interacting with life are taking shape. For instance, our body may naturally crave water in the morning, not as a conscious decision but as an instinctual signal for self-care after a night of fasting; this behavior becomes ingrained as a habitual response. Similarly, on a psychological level, when feeling emotionally drained, our body may seek tranquility. Over time, this repetitive approach to dealing with stress could shape the introverted aspect of our character.

During the transition from pregnancy to motherhood, significant changes occur in the woman's body, leading to a profound transformation of this primal layer. Whether experiencing morning sickness during pregnancy or extreme sleep deprivation after the baby is born, the body's responses to the new circumstances differ from those before. For instance, the simple act of drinking a glass of water may induce nausea, and there may be no opportunity for emotional recuperation during moments of stress as the baby requires physical contact with the mother's body. The woman's lower level of personality undergoes a profound shift as her volitions and instincts become intertwined with those of the new life she must learn to share her body with.

For Husserl, motivations stem from the daily routines shaped by the natural order of our bodies. The interconnected web of habits that gradually form the fundamental aspects of our personality creates a sense of comfort and familiarity in which we feel truly ourselves. This feeling of being at home in our own skin, known to the Stoics as "oikeiosis", is a sense of being in harmony with the habitual patterns we unconsciously repeat each day, guided by our lower instincts and emotions. However, during pregnancy and early motherhood, the old skin must be shed.

Indeed, habits serve as a primitive form of "association" that drives the lower layer of emotions to solidify raw experiences into a foundational character that shapes the core of our motivational life. As Husserl succinctly puts it, "The similar motivates the similar under similar circumstances" (Husserl, 2020, p. 236). In the context of the transition to early motherhood, this core set of habits that triggers motivational responses is not yet fully established, leading to a woman whose motivational life is still in flux due to the profound physiological changes her body is undergoing.

Her driving forces may not be readily apparent to her subjective awareness, yet they propel her toward new and unexpected paths. For instance, in the first trimester, she may feel unusually fatigued and hungry despite no visible changes in her body. Postpregnancy, her immune system may weaken, leading to unfamiliar health issues. Even seemingly simple tasks like brushing her teeth in the morning can become daunting for the new mother, driven by her primal instincts and emotional impulses. Under the surface, a more primal force is constantly influencing her motivations—the instinctual drive for the survival and well-being of her baby.

The organic matter of her body is shifting in a new and uncharted direction, driving toward meanings that have yet to take form. She may not understand why she chooses one behavior over another; a simple example is her sudden enjoyment of foods she previously disliked during pregnancy, possibly because they are nutritionally crucial for the baby's development.

According to Husserl, motivation does not primarily arise from volitions. We do not choose to want what we want; rather, our wants choose us and, if we allow them, propel us toward that sense of homeliness we experience when we are at ease in our own skin. Motivation is not inherently linked to volitions or the ego's objectives, as original motivation transcends the ego and belongs to this egoless layer of spirit. Motivation acts as a passive force that irrationally or pre-rationally moves the organic matter, influencing the biological body and transforming it into a subject. The foundational "law" (Husserl, 2020, p. 234) of motivation stems from this continuous drive to exist. We are motivated by our biological body (Koerper), a body distinct from our own, as it encounters nature and provides evidence that underpins our choices and values.

For instance, during the transition from pregnancy to early motherhood, the motivational core of both bodies flows within a shared organic matter, leading to conflicts over simple matters like the allocation of essential nutrients. The mother's body may require nutrients that are also crucial for the child during gestation.

However, it is in the spontaneous interaction with this flow that the body (Hua XXXVII, 114) senses an immediate feeling of rightness, which it perceives as truth. The woman believes she is making the right choice by eating a particular food because it feels satisfying to her. She values and finds meaning in consuming nutritious food primarily because of this sensation and only secondarily due to medical advice. This bodily (Leibhaftig) experienced authenticity recognizes the value itself—or what is perceived as true—as an immediate organic fact. "I know I am doing the right thing because it feels right".

As the woman navigates the ever-evolving balance between her own body and her baby's life, harmonizing within this shared organic realm, she discovers a sense of well-being. For instance, as a new mother, she may feel a sense of satisfaction when her child is peacefully asleep, well-fed and clean. The woman's new identity naturally regulates itself around her baby, even on a deeply organic level.

This forms the conceptual foundation of what I have termed symbiotic individuation. Both the mother and her baby will gradually differentiate their identities and newly formed set of habits from a common foundation of organic emotions. Their shared core of primal instincts and emotions guides them in similar directions, though the meanings and values they develop over time may diverge. As Merleau-Ponty notes in "Phenomenology of Perception" (1962, pp. XIV–XVII), this encounter unveils to us our essence and our concept of truth or validity. Through this interaction, I can delve into the depths of my self-awareness.

During the transition from pregnancy to the period of exterogestation spanning up to 18 months after birth, an ongoing interplay between the woman's body and that of the baby unfolds a revealing connection that exposes the woman to the self-revealing truth of her future self. It is the shared organic substance of her emerging body that propels her motivational drive and will in a new direction that is unfamiliar to her as well. She learns about herself and her evolving body through the gradual development of the baby's body over time. This encounter signifies the emergence of a fresh dimension of her emotional consciousness (Hua XXXVII, 117), which serves as the a priori condition (Hua XXXVII, 118, 115) for any action that feels right and secure.

III.1   I Am, You Are

The new role that a woman assumes after pregnancy requires her to awaken her subjectivity to a new set of desires and motivations. In order to embrace this role as both the person she is and the person she is becoming, she must integrate all aspects of herself. This involves actively participating in shaping the meanings that emerge on an organic level. According to Husserl, at this level, the organic essence of life transforms into an "I" that acts over time to manifest its core habits and behaviors (Hua XXXVII, 104). As human beings, we strive to achieve wholeness. Our various components seek a unity that is not inherently singular but rather interconnected and co-constituted.

For new mothers, the challenges of "brain fog", changes in body shape, the contrast with their former selves, the overwhelming sense of love, and the tranquility felt when their baby is asleep—all of these are fragmented elements struggling to find coherence, particularly when faced with their past selves. This struggle is compounded by the swift changes that characterize this phase. The lower stratum of the body lacks the time to establish a stable foundation of affection, as both the mother's body and the baby's body undergo rapid transformations. This can be an immensely disorienting experience, akin to the swift transition from infancy to puberty within a short span of 18 months. The mother's body seeks to comprehend these changes, yet finding unity and harmony among the rapidly shifting components proves to be a significant challenge.

In contrast to the lower level, at this higher level, motivations intertwine with the ego in the pursuit of creating a cohesive whole through interconnected and interdependent expectations. Consequently, the motivational journey of a new mother involves a continual reorganization that must adapt to each change in both her body and her baby's body. Both bodies veer in unforeseen directions from what she had grown accustomed to, leaving her uncertain about the demands of motherhood. Her entire being is not yet fully her own, not even in the realm of expectations, let alone habits or intentions. Activities she once performed effortlessly may now present challenges.

As previously mentioned, Husserl posits that there are inherent laws within the natural course of our existence that organize matter into a uniform and cohesive core. This innate necessity or immediate sense of rightness, which the body perceives through spontaneous interactions with its material self, sets off a series of reactions that transform the initially indistinct flow of being into a unified entity we eventually recognize as the self and its sense-making activity (Hua XXXVII, 102). A new mother may feel this sense of rightness when breastfeeding her child, witnessing the peace that her body's nourishment brings—a wholly new organic experience, especially in the case of first-time pregnancies. The interaction between her body and her child's is novel, and her own body feels unfamiliar to her. Consequently, she is still discovering the capabilities of her body within her lived reality, guided by the non-aliud—that which is connected to her and reveals to her what she is becoming through each bodily encounter. It may seem as though the woman cannot fully grasp her subjectivity and her ability to make sense of the organic changes affecting her life; this understanding will gradually emerge through each encounter.

At this level, subjective bodies are motivated as mere functions for various forms of consciousness (Hua XXXVII, 101): emotional, logical, practical and others. The diverse organic demands that impact the ego shape it functionally, giving rise to different facets of the self. Each action carries what Husserl terms propositions—efforts to recapture and clarify the immediate sense of evidence and truthfulness experienced by consciousness in prior encounters (Hua XXX-VII, 118). Motivation at this stage pertains to what the ego deems right; however, during transitions, much of the unfolding and clarification of sense is new and often perplexing. To render this unfolding comprehensible, the woman must engage in a daily practice of attending to her bodily experiences, regardless of how minor they may seem: the morning hunger, the evening muscle soreness, the desire for a walk and so forth. These organic experiences can be elevated to a predictive level and evolve into propositions that yield new meanings and further determinations. The sense of rightness and feeling of comfort in one's own skin, derived from assigning meaning to these experiences, are encountered through an intelligible process in which the motivational force transforms from something egoless into something reflexive, introspective and personal.

III.2 A New Skin

Our motivations and volitional lives are the skin where we find peace and refuge to be ourselves. According to Husserl, our volitional life is not guided by our ego, which dictates how our skin should feel and what we should feel motivated to do. Motivations are not psychological acts; rather, they are essential laws of nature that drive our volitional bodies to decide upon their actions (Hua XXX-VII, 89). By volitional body, I mean the mind-body unity that constitutes the primal decisional layer of our being. This volitional body represents an ethical subject, an en-worlded person exercising her will and choices.

The essential rightness and contingency of nature are felt by the body and translated into a set of embodied norms that are taken as the horizon of normality, on the basis of which persons make their decisions and reinforce their habits (Hua XXXVII, 89). As mentioned earlier, those decisions stem from a motivational force that is organic, impersonal and bodily. Meanwhile, on a higher layer, it is reflective, personal and normative, and it impinges on the body in a constitutive way. An example of these two motivational layers as applied to a breastfeeding mother is as follows:

1. My body is enjoying a lentil soup.
2. I realize that I am eating lentil soup, and I should not do it because I risk causing my baby painful colics.

In this example, the egoless layer encounters the reflective subjective one, revealing a conflict between the organic matter and the subjective will of the newly constituted I. The mother's body might need iron and feel the desire to eat lentil soup, but her reflective subject understands that fulfilling this need could be harmful to her primary goal, which is the peaceful survival of her baby. Clearly, being constantly alert to such decisions creates overstimulation that can be very draining for a new mother.

The two levels of motivation—the bodily and the reflective—represent the a priori condition for the individual to act practically and theoretically in the world (Hua XXXVII, 89). Husserl writes, "I want the means because I am motivated by wanting the premises" (Hua XXXVII, 88). Motivation is what allows for rational determinations and practical decisions. It connects an essence to the normative level. On the one hand, the organic body takes what it wants; on the other, the subject that awakens in that body decides what to do based on what its volitional body resolves is best.

III.3 Operating and Not-Operating Willing

Our will is a driving force that moves from the organic to the more subjective layers of our being.[1] As Husserl teaches in his lectures, willing is the practical motivational force underlying any conscious field. As a subjective faculty, it properly belongs to the person exercising it, but it can only be activated by the lower organic matter, or, so to speak, the force of nature.

To describe this dynamic, Husserl distinguishes three forms of willing acts: the resolve (Vorsatz), the fiat and the action-will (Handlungswille). Regarding the action-will, it can be further divided into operating and non-operating willing (Hua XXVIII, 118). Operating will is a form of procedural will that does not yet know what it is about to decide. This is the kind of will operating in the volitional body during the transition from pregnancy to motherhood, where there is no precise aiming at actual achievements but simply being according to the pregnancy and its course. The transition from operating will into action-will more accurately describes the state of pregnancy, where the woman becomes a subject despite and because of the non-aliud that motivates the transformation. This form of volition is not aimed at an actual achievement based on a cognitive level; it is not, "I want to become bigger, hence I will have a baby". The operating will is at work when my "I" is just emerging from the realm of passivity and becoming a subject; that is, a belly is growing and a body is changing. That belly and that body are mine. The baby will be born when they are ready. Only when the body's operating will is ready will I be able to take ownership of it and fulfill its resolve in bringing new life into the world. Hence, I will be able to push to help that life grow outside of me.

Or, to use the earlier example, I notice that my body is eating something I should avoid during breastfeeding, and I realize that my body might need iron that I should provide in other ways. Only after that awakening does the operating will become an action-will, in which my "I" is aware of the goal that my living volitional body wants to achieve (Hua XXVIII, 118).

Practical possibilities always relate to a subject who can desire them (Hua XXVIII, 122). Tendency, attention and interest are the three movements of the mind-body unit that explicate the transition from operating will to action-will, from a lower spiritual level to a higher one. Initially, as stated before, the "I" is just receptive. In receptivity, although the ego is indeed actively turned toward what affects it, it does not make its knowledge and the individual steps of cognition an object of will (Husserl, 1973, p. 198). The receptive activity creates a horizon of apprehending attention that modifies the structure of the not-yet-I into a tension, meaning the "I" tendens ad (stretching toward) its object. In that sense, meditation or simple exercises of mindful presence can help strengthen receptivity toward the non-aliud underlying the motivational transformation of the woman. Developing attention to what the body is doing can help in becoming that body and encountering its operating will.

In general, attention is a tending of the ego toward an intentional object, toward a unity which appears continually in the change of the modes of its givens ... it is a tending toward realization.

(Husserl, 1973, p. 80)

As shown in the quotation, attention is a physical tension that can be accepted or denied by the subject aware of it. Noticing a preference for new foods, paying attention to mood fluctuations and being mindful of new areas of pain can all be actions that, if not dismissed, can increase a woman's ownership of her body and her action-will. If this tension is accepted through mindful presence and then enhanced by the "I", it becomes interest; this interest allows the "I" to actually participate in the object and transform the act of tension into an act of apprehension. Taking an interest in one's own life, from the smallest spontaneous acts to the most complex ones, can be a way to clarify the structure of the non-aliud and regain insight into the motivational force driving a woman's body during the transition. Through the support of attention and interest, the will operates in an objectifying way—that is, in the attempt to grasp its object, it fixes its predicative and practical identity according to what is given in that moment.

III.4 Desires Need Time to Become Willing

How can we know when our volitions are fulfilled? How can we distinguish them from mere desires? Time and willing are intrinsically connected. According to the unfolding of time, an intention can either develop into a willing or remain a mere desire. If an intention aims at realization, it can be considered a form of willing; if it does not manifest in anything concrete, it remains a desire. For Husserl, willing is closely tied to time because it is through time that an intention becomes will rather than remaining just a desire or a wish. Husserl asserts (in Hua-Mat IX, 133 or Hua XXVIII, 103–12) that willing aims at practical realization; otherwise, a volition would not be a volition but simply a desire.[2]

The basic characteristic of any volition is its possibility to be achieved (Erreichenbarkeit). While willing something is the practical analogon of certitude and it can be modified according to hypotheses or disjunctive modifications of willing (Hua XXVIII, 127), desire is the practical analogon of the question (here we mean "question" in the Latin sense of the word *quaero*, that is, asking a question without any expectation to receive an answer in return). Wanting something means that my will is certain to be able to reach its wanted object in the future (Hua XXVIII, 121–2). In a new mother's life, this certitude is denied even for actions as small as standing up to get a glass of water. According to Husserl, the future is the field of the concrete achievement of the volition. Volition's goals can be fulfilled and find their concretization only in the future; before that the volition is achieved they exist only as ideals (Hua XXVIII, 123). In that sense, volitions are creative acts (i.e. they create something), while desires are tendencies that arise in the present and tend toward the future without posing the future as certain. Thus, a day in a mother's life can be shaped by a set of inclinations that may never materialize into practical actions. What is conceived as an action may simply remain as an inclination and a longing from the past—for instance, desiring a glass of water but remaining seated on the couch breastfeeding the baby. Parenthetically, it is worth noting the crucial importance of water for a breastfeeding mother. If she finds herself alone on the couch, do not assume that she wants to be left undisturbed. Kindly inquire if she needs anything, as she may refrain from moving or speaking to avoid disturbing the baby, yet she could very well be in need of something as basic and essential as a glass of water.

In the transition to motherhood, the distinction between volitions and desires becomes blurred. What is wanted may be posited as an attainable goal for the future but may be compromised by the demands of the upcoming. From the simple act of getting dressed and clean in the morning to the more complex endeavor of returning to a beloved job, the new maternal body must adapt to forming habits that often conflict with pre-existing personal inclinations.

The volitional structure of a woman's body may not fully support the motivational drive that propels her spirit through the chain of realizations over time. Consequently, the transition from resolve to action—moving from intention to implementation—is not always achievable. In this context, the process of becoming a subject proves to be quite challenging, as the motivational force behind the formation of new habits and personal identity may take unexpected turns. The woman might become someone she does not yet recognize or expect, as the outcomes of her will may diverge from her initial expectations.

Therefore, it can be very helpful to focus on achievable resolutions, no matter how small they may seem, such as taking a daily shower, getting dressed or going for a walk outside. These small resolutions represent the emerging core of habits that will gradually shape her new identity, from which a renewed motivational force can exert its influence.

Unlike joy or desire, volitions are always directed toward what is real; they are excluded from the ideal sphere and the past (Hua XXVIII, 123). Volition encompasses not only the present and its creator but also the subsequent temporal extension and its content. Willing is expressed in the present through its creative fiat but tends toward the future, aiming to realize its goal through action (Hua XXVIII, 125). Creative realization can only occur when reality emerges or when we are unaware of its presence, as it originates from nothing—the non-aliud (Hua XXVIII, 126). From this nothingness, or the "not other" growing within her womb, a woman's new identity forms through volitions that become concrete over time.

During the transition to motherhood, some of the woman's previous aspirations may not be fully realized; they remain mere wishes, hidden in the non-aliud of her existence. Ultimately, she may come to see her old identity as just a wish, potentially leading to frustration and a depressive core.

Volitions require reality, and reality needs the future to come into being (Hua XXVIII, 122). Willing begins in the present but always refers to the chain of protentions and retentions, which bring the act into existence in the future. The present desires of a pregnant woman might not be realized in her future role as a mother, as a different person with new habits will be there to enact those volitions. For instance, a woman might desire an active social life with her child, but as a new mother, she may lack the energy and organizational capacity to make that a reality. Moreover, the being growing inside her may have different motivations both in the womb and after birth. The baby's volitions might differ from the mother's on both lower and higher levels. The baby's needs—such as requiring nighttime care, constant holding or being fussy during walks—may necessitate practical adjustments that clash with the mother's motivations. Volitions are inherently future-oriented, always referring to what has yet to be created (Hua X, 26)—the non-aliud. Here, the non-aliud remains an enigmatic source of existence that must unfold in the future, but without a strong motivational force from the mother, as her subjectivity is influenced by the challenging bodily motivational logic shared with the baby.

The thesis of willing pertains not only to the present and its creative inception but also to the future, which makes willing an operative and positive force (Hua XXVIII, 125). The future becomes the non-aliud through which the identities of the mother and her child unfold.

IV. A Broken Narrative

It has been suggested that middle pregnancy typically represents a time of introspection (Gloger-Tippelt, 1983; Shereshefsky & Yarrow, 1973). In fact, the woman is going to take a maternal role (Miller, 2005) whose meaning and value are not yet filled with personal meaning and value but are mostly referred to what this role means in the society and for others (Uriko, 2019; Yopo Díaz, 2018). The acquisition of motherhood has been defined mostly on standards developed in the 1950s and 1970s (Rubin, 1984), which fail to reflect the social changes developed after the civil rights movements in the late 1960s (Fouquier, 2011). Especially when holding a woman-centered perspective which takes into account the image of the woman not just at the mercy of their hormones but it sticks to the interpretation of subjective reality as experienced by her (Nicolson, 1986, p. 146, italics in original), it is possible to see how the motivational effort that guides the volitional life of the woman during this transition seems to be so to speak blind. The non-operating will cannot count on very few positions of certitude that can be fulfilled in the future through the fiat of the operating will because she does not know yet how the core habit of her future character will look like. Therefore, the thesis posed in the present is challenged in its fiat in the future.

While in many transitions that occur in one's life, we are guided by role models or motivational goals that are in sight (the transition from school to a job, from bachelor life to marriage etc.), in the transition to early motherhood, there is a biological and psychological revolution comparable to transformations such as puberty, menopause or recoveries after impairing diseases. In becoming a mother, women must reevaluate their autonomy, physical appearance and capability, sexuality, their occupation and influence on their sphere of existence (Nicolson, 1999).

Hence, the motivational force blindly moves in search of a new shape to take. As Ibarra's and colleague's qualitative study (2010) shows, women observe role models and try to identify potential similarities between them and the new identity they are trying to form, but as the interviewees remark, certain identities felt unreal and expressed in comments such as "no, this just isn't me" or "I balance between who I am and what society expects me to be", since a culturally accepted discourse facilitates the granting of identity (Ibarra & Barbulescu, 2010). The *non-aliud* is what against which the motivational force shapes the coming identity of the new mother in unexpected directions. As Grant and colleagues (2015) remark, fixed narratives can become a trap in which the woman keeps narrating to herself a story that does not mirror her actual feeling of the moment. It might be, in fact, that the smile of her baby can repay her of everything in a moment, but if she has been sleepless and poorly nourished for months, the smile of her baby can be a sweet parenthesis in the midst of a heavily foggy day.

On average, scholars observed that women with a higher education who are strongly motivated by the job they feel passionate about are most likely to express the intention to work full-time after the birth of their child and found in their job a line of continuity with their identity (Merens et al., 2011). Yet, as we saw earlier, it is not clear if this continuity would be sustained by the lower bodily motivation of the woman's body. She might be wanting so but that will might remain a frustrated tendency. Although some scholars believed that it is possible to develop one's identity independently from others (see Cattell, 1943; Erikson, 1950; Freud, 1961), in accordance with other scholars, I believe that the relational aspect of our identity is extremely important in shaping who we are (Chodorow, 1978; Gilligan, 1982; Josselson, 1987), especially when going through the experience of pregnancy where no clear boundaries determine where the woman ends and the baby begins. In the transition from pregnancy to motherhood, women must modify their understandings of themselves and who they are in relationship to other people (Steinberg, 2005).

IV.1   First-Hand Accounts

To conclude this chapter, I would like to provide brief passages of mothers' self-reflections on their capacity to act according to their volitions. Nicolson's (1999) study evidenced how women felt let down by their partners:

> I still felt resentful. I felt that once he'd gone out through that door then he didn't have to think about it until he came back through the door. . . . When he went off in the morning his life hadn't changed. It was the same as

the day after we had her. It was the same as the day before we had her. But everything for me had just gone completely, you know, up in the air. Everything was different.

(1999, pp. 635–642)

The transition is so profound that it resembles a loss of identity. No new identity is clearly in sight during this transformation, and there is certainly no way to return to the previous one. The mother's basic instincts and needs are now aligned with those of the baby, and she is the one responsible for accommodating them, as illustrated in Patricia's story:

Sex was planned, if it happened at all, during her naps and once in awhile we would go on date night. Everything was scheduled in little boxes of time between her naps and feedings and the nanny and work. Nothing spontaneous at all and it all functioned best if I just accommodated everyone's needs. We didn't have a ton of money and the grandparents were either too old or too far away to be much help. If I wanted to sleep in or eat late or not stop at the park or talk for awhile with a friend or whatever, I would be penalized by crying and whining, which was hard to tolerate. Children find a way to get their needs met and it felt to me like a mainline into my heart. So I put myself aside in many ways for years.

As one mother recounts, giving up on so much of yourself feels like a loss of identity:

'It almost feels like a loss of self at the beginning with the first child, just because newborns basically need you 24=7 [all day, every day].'

(1998, p. 638)

I just felt so lost and felt like I had no identity at all anymore.

(1998, p. 641)

The blindness of the motivational force guiding this transition echoes the sense of loss that women experience when becoming mothers. This is because the motivational force shaping their personality becomes deeply intertwined and connected with that of their children. As one woman reflected on mothering, she said,

I think it has added to my person, I wouldn't say I'm a totally different person, but it has changed me. I think at the core I am still who I am, but it definitely added to [my person].

(1998, p. 642)

Or in Nina's story:

> I love watching my daughters grow up and being able to accompany them in their development. I love being their mom. As the children become more independent, I have more time and space for myself again, which I greatly appreciate and which does me good. I am glad to have a very interesting and fulfilling profession and, in addition to the beautiful but demanding family life of five, to have other aspects of life. I enjoy being independent again, experiencing something alone with my husband, and being able to tackle my own projects again. And I enjoy it every time I come home and my three daughters tell me with glowing eyes what moves them and what they have experienced. I am excited to see where our journey as a family and my journey as a mother and woman will take us.

For some women, the end phase of this transition can be considered a form of "expanded consciousness", where they incorporate their children into their intrapsychic boundaries or even fuse their lives with them. Some of them write that they grew so attuned to their children's lives that they could oftentimes anticipate their children's needs even when the children were not immediately present. In that sense, the problem of identity in the transition is not resolved but transferred to the being of the baby, who consequently, with time, might encounter problems in expressing its own identity. In fact, as shown in Nicolson's study (1999), some women resolve the blindness in sight of their transition and the impasse evidenced in the Aristotelian logic by fusing their own experience with their children's experiences, thus hindering any symbiotic individuation. Yet, as time progresses, the lower motivational force helps the organic differentiation of the two beings, and it becomes easier for women to see the difference that ignites self-reflection on the core of habits that will form the new interrelated identities. As in Elliott's story:

> I have instilled in my children that family is defined as those that give identity and security and who you give the same in return. Others that are bound to you by blood or legal status are relatives. This definition has given me comfort that there is still a role in sharing identity and security, but I am no longer the primary person to do that. The continued human development that is my life now means that I must go back to the skills I learned in parenting my children. The self-reparenting experience starts again. I must unpack who I am now and who I am evolving to be. There is a constant challenge of what being the parent of adult children is going to be as compared to an adult that is making choices with myself as the primary stakeholder. There is a persistent exploration of who I want to be as a fully formed being that is not spending most of my time and resources on dependents. My sense of connectedness to

my adults [I don't call them my kids anymore] looks and feels different and that can be challenging for me—and that is my work to do now.

Or, in this other story, a woman reflected on her awareness of her son's uniqueness:

As they get older they become more of a person, there's a lot more reflection about different personalities and how God's made us all different. [I'm] learning to appreciate my son and his unique personality and gifts and weaknesses, [learning to] appreciate all that.

As described by Rotkirch and Janhunen (2010), another dynamic that emerges during the transition, where the motivational force operates at a pre-personal level in both beings, is the feeling of being divided and depleted (2010, p. 97). This feeling reflects the conflict between the organic motivational forces of the two interconnected bodies. What the child wants and what the mother can provide do not always align. For instance, the mother may want to breastfeed her child but might not have enough milk supply, or she may wish to be more attentive and energetic but often feels exhausted. It is in this lack of alignment that the operating and non-operating wills of both mother and child can evolve into an action-oriented will, generating a new core of habits from which their distinct personalities will develop and individuate. As another woman recounts:

The oneyear- old sometimes wants to be in my arms all evening. My husband is home from work and I finally try to get for instance some housework done. Then I get irritated over having to carry the child all the time. . . . After a few minutes I feel shame and self-loathing.

In Maren's story, we can clearly see how, even if the motivation is present, we often have no chance to act on it according to our own will. The flourishing of our baby becomes a prevailing motivational force that overrides our basic volitions:

Before, I usually worked late hours, on weekends, and took holidays to work on articles or book projects. This is not possible anymore, every evening colloquium with drinks, every late meeting, conference, workshop or talk abroad must be planned months ahead and negotiated with the working agenda of your partner. Going for a conference (mostly on Fridays and Saturdays), means that your partner either has to take vacation (to accompany you) or stay the whole weekend at home with your child and has no time left for whatsoever (as baby's up to 2 or 3 years do not occupy themselves, but want to be entertained and accompany you even when you have to visit the bathroom.:-). Getting this time from your partner, means thus that they will miss time for themselves, and that you will in turn get less leisure time, i.e., time to spend for yourself or with friends. To make a long story short. Even in the most ideal circumstances, you end up with nearly no time for either research or yourself, while continuously hearing from (mostly) male colleagues: ah we don't see you around anymore so often, it is probably because you are "mothering" now, want to be with your child all the time, and philosophy and meeting colleagues is less important to you.

No, I am not so much around, because I have to use all the time I get as effectively as possible, and thus have no time for chitchat, drinking coffee or lunch with colleagues or even go for drinks after a seminar, not because I do not want to or would enjoy it, but simply because otherwise everything would fall apart, my work, my daily arrangements, and my relationship.

As LeBeau (2014, p. 95) notes, mothers might even feel divided and guilty when they try to meet their own needs, as it takes time away from their children. On the other hand, children, especially around the age of two, often say "no" more frequently to differentiate themselves from their caregivers. Attending to one's own needs is one of the few, yet sometimes painful, ways to exercise one's operating and action-will, allowing one to stay connected to their core habits. For mothers, this is essential for letting their new identity thrive. Another woman says:

I felt guilty for wanting to do other things than take care of my baby because she needs me so much. How selfish of me to want to be productive instead of taking care of this helpless child.

Or in Maren's story:

The first day, we brought Emma to the day care after 4 months, although difficult at first, because I felt kind of guilty, was such a relief. I came home and the first thing I did was sleeping for two hours. Being back at work slowly gave me back my old confidence and identity, and I turned into a much more relaxed and sovereign mother, at last. Now, I was looking forward to spending time with my baby, no longer overwhelmed and chained to my home. Also, little Emma developed a much steadier rhythm, slept better, and cried less, after she went to day care from Monday to Wednesday, and on Thursdays spend the day with her grandma. On Fridays, my partner took care of her, as he took parental leave in the first year (and I in the second year).

The sense of guilt, depletion and feeling divided seems to be part of the unfolding of the non-aliud, which allows a woman to get closer to her new self. This process, akin to Hegel's concept of Aufhebung, still conserves the traces of the oppositions within her—her being and not being, her old self and her new child. From my perspective, if the transitional phase of motherhood is not successful—if the lower and higher motivational forces remain in a blind spot where the will cannot become operative in time—the risk is falling into what Butler (1990) called performative gender identity. This could lead to a fusion that does not allow both identities to grow and individuate.

If a woman does not know how to resolve the willpower driving her motivational forces in time, the ideology connected to women is reinforced and perpetuated. According to Butler, we perform our gender through behaviors that are socially perceived as appropriate and consistent. This social conditioning replaces the operating will and prevents us from discovering our true selves. Thus, performing gender, as Butler (1988) describes, is "reiterative" and not entirely a choice, given the societal retributions for not conforming to one's gender.

V. Conclusion

In this chapter, I focused on the problem of motivation and volition during pregnancy and early motherhood. Volitions are not driven by our subjectivity but are moved by a more primal force. Their realization over time is what distinguishes actual volition from mere tendencies or desires.

Motivation originates as an organic force that propels the body into repeated habits, forming our character and personality. It operates on two layers: an organic layer and willpower. The organic layer can be described as the sheer force of nature in which we participate not as subjects but as bodies trying to make sense of their needs. In this sense, the organic structure of the mother encompasses a "non aliud"—a mysterious "not other" that unfolds in the mother's life and affects her symbiotic individuation from her child. The logic involved in this unfolding challenges our understanding of the creation of subjectivity over time. The woman does not yet know what her body wants or will realize in time. Thus, to allow symbiotic individuation to occur, the formation of her subjectivity over time is continuously challenged by the interpretive obscurity of her organic matter.

The main proposal from this interpretation of the motivational layers of this lived experience is for the woman to take an interest in her own life without forcing the understanding of the motivational force. Additionally, she should exert her willpower (resolve, fiat and action) as much as possible, even in small actions. The combination of both efforts would contribute to the creation of a core set of habits that reinforces both lower and higher motivational forces, from which a renewed identity will emerge.

Despite the seeming illogic of having children, as it contradicts the logical frameworks we are accustomed to—especially those explaining the functioning of our bodies—it remains the most striking expression of the mystery of life, the "non aliud", which obeys neither our will nor our brain. It is an ongoing transformation that drives the survival of being.

Notes

1 In his lectures on ethics and value theory (1914), Husserl writes that "The will . . . takes part in the more general sphere of pure reason . . . the specific and pregnant meaning of will refers solely to a particular kind of activity that underpins all the other fields of consciousness. . . . It seems even more evident that the will . . . is a particular and superior form of activity that can come into play everywhere under some essential conditions that lie in objectivations and in presupposed sentiments" (Husserl XXX-VIII, p. 68; cf. also Hua XXXI, pp. 9–10).
2 "When we distinguish two levels of interest and, corresponding to these, two levels of objectifying operations, viz. that belonging to receptive experience, on the one hand, and that of predicative spontaneity, on the other, this distinction of levels should not be construed as if the different operations were somehow separate from each other" (Husserl, 1973, p. 203).

References

Aristotle. (350 B.C.). *Metaphysics* (W. D. Ross, Trans.). The Internet Classics Archive. Retrieved June 10, 2020, from http://classics.mit.edu/Aristotle/metaphysics.4.iv.html
Bornemark, J. (2023). The logic of pregnancy. *The Journal of Medicine and Philosophy: A Forum for Bioethics and Philosophy of Medicine*, 48(2), 128–140.
Butler, J. (1988). Performative acts and gender constitution: An essay in phenomenology and feminist theory. *Theatre Journal*, 40(4), 519–531.
Cattell, R. B. (1943). The description of personality: Basic traits resolved into clusters. *Journal of Abnormal and Social Psychology*, 38, 476–506.
Chodorow, N. J. (1978). *The reproduction of mothering: Psychoanalysis and the sociology of gender*. University of California Press.
Erikson, E. H. (1950). *Childhood and society*. Norton.
Ettinger, B. (2006a). *The matrixial borderspace*. University of Minnesota Press.
Ettinger, B. (2006b). From proto-ethical compassion to responsibility: Besideness and the three primal mother-phantasies of not-enoughness, devouring and abandonment. *Athena*, 2.
Fouquier, K. F. (2011). The concept of motherhood among three generations of African American women. *Journal of Nursing Scholarship*, 43(2), 145–153.
Freud, S. (1961). *The ego and the id*. Norton.
Gilligan, C. (1982). *In a different voice: Psychological theory and women's development*. Harvard University Press.
Gloger-Tippelt, G. (1983). A process model of the pregnancy course. *Human Development*, 26(3), 134–148.
Grant, A., Leigh-Phippard, H., & Short, N. (2015). Re-storying narrative identity: A dialogical study of mental health recovery and survival. *Journal of Psychiatric and Mental Health Nursing*, 22.
Hine, R. H., Maybery, D. J., & Goodyear, M. J. (2019). Identity in personal recovery for mothers with a mental illness. *Frontiers in Psychiatry*, 10, 89.
Husserl, E. (1970). *Crisis of European sciences and transcendental phenomenology* (D. Carr, Ed.). Northwestern Press. (Husserliana VI)
Husserl, E. (1973). *Zur Phänomenologie der Intersubjektivität. Texte aus dem Nachlass. Zweiter Teil: 1921–1928*. Husserliana, vol. XIV (Hua XIV) (I. Kern, Ed.). Martinus Nijhoff.
Husserl, E. (2020). *Studien zur Struktur des Bewusstseins, Teilband III. Wille und Handlung Teilband III. Wille und Handlung. Text aus dem Nachlass (1902–1934)* (U. Melle & T. Vongehr Ed.). Springer. (Husserlaina XLIII/3)

Ibarra, H., & Barbulescu, R. (2010). Identity as narrative: Prevalence, effectiveness, and consequences of narrative identity work in macro role transitions. *Academy of Management Review*, *35*(1), 135–154.

Josselson, R. (1987). *Finding herself: Pathways to identity development in women.* Jossey-Bass/Wiley.

Laney, E., Hall, M., Anderson, T., & Willingham, M. (2015). Becoming a mother: The influence of motherhood on women's identity development. *Identity*, *15*, 126–145.

LeBeau, C. S. (2014). *Maternal guilt: An existential phenomenological study of the early experiences of first-time mothers* (AAI3558815). PsycINFO database. 1508429832; 2014-99040-395.

Lewis, A. (1951). *An interesting condition.* Odhams.

Merens, A., Van den Brakel, M., Hartgers, M., & Hermans, B. (2011). *Emancipatiemonitor 2010.* Sociaal en Cultureel Planbureau, Centraal Bureau voor de Statistiek.

Merleau-Ponty, M. (1962). *Phenomenology of perception* (C. Smith, Trans.). Routledge.

Miller, T. (2005). *Making sense of motherhood: A narrative approach.* Cambridge University Press.

Montagu, A. (1961). Neonatal and infant immaturity in man. *JAMA*, *178*(1), 56–57.

Nicolson, P. (1986). Developing a feminist approach to depression following childbirth. In S. Wilkinson (Ed.), *Feminist social psychology: Developing theory and practice.* Open University Press.

Nicolson, P. (1999). Loss, happiness, and postpartum depression: The ultimate paradox. *Canadian Psychology*, *40*, 162–178.

Razurel, C., Bruchon-Schweitzer, M., Dupanloup, A. (2011). Stressful events, social support and coping strategies of primiparous women during the postpartum period: A qualitative study. *Midwifery*, *27*(2), 237–242.

Rich, A. (1977). *Of woman born.* Virago.

Rotkirch, A., & Janhunen, K. (2010). Maternal guilt. *Evolutionary Psychology*, *8*(1), 90–106.

Rubin, R. (1984). *Maternal identity and the maternal experience.* Springer Publishing.

Shereshefsky, P. M., & Yarrow, L. J. (Eds.). (1973). *Psychological aspects of a first pregnancy and early postnatal adaptation.* Raven Press.

Steinberg, Z. (2005). Donning the mask of motherhood: A defensive strategy, a developmental search. *Studies in Gender and Sexuality*, *6*, 173–198.

Uriko, K. (2019). Dialogical self and the changing body during the transition to motherhood. *Journal of Constructivist Psychology*, *32*(3), 221–235.

Yopo Díaz, M. (2018). Enacting motherhood: Time and social change in Chile. *Journal of Gender Studies*, *27*(4), 411–427.

Ziebart, K. M. (2013). *Nicolaus Cusanus on faith and the intellect: A case study in 15th-century fides-ratio controversy.* Brill.

5

MORE GOSSIP, LESS ETHICS

Ethics of Motherhood and Self-Transformations

I. Introduction: The Outcasts

I am sitting here by myself on an intercontinental flight that carries me back to my family after three days of conference in Europe. Behind me, a 10-month-old child has been crying for almost the entire trip. People barely tolerate him, and the mother looks grim in her face, exhausted, mad. As I am writing about motherhood, I feel unease to carry on with my writing while some practical help is needed. I try to catch the mother's attention in case she needs some help. I speak to her. She does not even notice it. She looks just desperate. Her husband seems mad and powerless. The baby keeps crying as any normal baby would if trapped in a small space for hours.

The point is that birth is an event that concerns all of us, although it often appears to be just a woman's problem. Instead, we seem to be barely tolerating it when it is not pleasant or looking cute. While society as a whole benefits from well-raised children, the emotional, physical and financial costs of raising them fall primarily on their families, particularly mothers. How we enter this world, grow connections in it and become the daughters and sons of someone is a very delicate intersubjective and interaffective problem.

From my perspective, it goes against any reasonable evidence to believe, as Moustakas (1961) and Wells (1984)[1] do, that we are born alone. To begin with, our conception stems from the biological and emotional bond between two individuals. One of them bears the growth of our being in her womb, and it is through her efforts that we come into this world. Afterwards, our emotional and physical growth is highly dependent on the intersubjective and interaffective connection we establish with these people and the environment in which we grow.

DOI: 10.4324/9781003490937-5

Nevertheless, a structural problem persists that emphasizes societal blindness toward the intersubjective quality of this phenomenon. In fact, we frequently interpret this phenomenon as if the mother is the only one truly responsible for the birth and development of her baby. We almost tend to confuse her with her baby to the point that they both become outcasts waiting at the edge of society to be ready to be accepted. Reintegration often happens through school when the mother gains more time for herself while her baby is at school and the baby gains new developmental tools outside the shared world with her mother. Yet, this reintegration might happen too late for her well-being; the stories collected in the first chapter speak loud about the sense of isolation in the first months of the baby's life. From here, it follows implicit societal rules such as a mother is not supposed to fly with her baby—what was she thinking? I heard someone say on this flight. She is not supposed to go to a restaurant or to go shopping with her baby (even groceries are sometimes considered a zone of danger considering how difficult it is to push a cart if you have two babies). She is expected to live as an outcast until the baby becomes tolerable for society, rather than society making itself more tolerable for the new life and her parents. Moreover, even when integration occurs, societal life is organized in such a way that we ask parents to come back to their working lives as if nothing has ever changed in their lives. For both the mother and the father, coming back to work implicitly requires coming back to the old version of themselves when the baby was not there with and for us. We ask them to be fresh, professional and, if necessary, unempathetic. At work, we need to function as we used to, as if the baby was never born. Even if the mother stays at home to take care of the children because her salary might be lower than her partner's or she cannot afford daycare, the sleeping arrangement might be adjusted so that the father sleeps in a separate room. This allows him to be fully functional at work, as if he is not involved in parenting. Being able to be fresh at work is often seen as more pressing than having the woman well rested while taking care of the baby(ies)—as if a sleep-deprived mother would not be a danger for herself and her children. These draining dynamics remain a private matter that should not be part of the societal organization of life, which should continue to flow as normal. In the long run, this reveals to be exhausting for both men and women and does not facilitate a harmonious life in society. Unhappy parents will raise unhappy children who will grow into troubled adults whose functioning in society might require extra support in order to be flourishing for both them and the society.

From my point of view, having a baby involves a deep intersubjective transformation that should be accommodated and understood at a societal level. Since we are all born, we all should care about the way in which we enter this world and develop in it; ignoring this intersubjective process creates a problematic unbalance that affects everyone's development in life. Understanding it can enrich our lives with more caring solutions, uplifting one's psychological distress.

Henceforth, in this chapter, I am going to discuss how the transition from pregnancy to early motherhood discloses a locus of embodied intersubjectivity that has the power of transforming us into children of someone else. This transformation has the peculiarity of being immanently transcendent. That is, while the woman transcends herself in this effort of expressing one of her biological reproductive goals, the product of her transcendence is not other than her but is corporeally related to her. To prove this point, I will highlight the double intentionality and the form of embodied empathy that characterizes this sort of transcendence. Following the steps of Heinämaa (2014), I do not believe that pregnancy indicates a fusion (Young, 1985) or a split subjectivity of mother and child (Ruddick, 1989), but I see this moment as the creation of new boundaries where a form of self-transformation takes place that is deeply embedded in the woman's body. In this transformative process, the woman decides or refutes to become the mother of the life she brought into this world.

Accordingly, the chapter aims at describing some of the key moments of this self-transformation and to understand how we perceive the other from this very close I-thou relationship. My theory is that the transformation occurring during the transition from pregnancy to early motherhood establishes the boundaries of a form of embodied intersubjectivity that is operative for the rest of our lives. That creates the footprint of how we will function in our life. Different from other forms of empathetic acts and intersubjective connections, the woman transforming into a mother becomes once and for all an embodied space of co-*Existenz* that even death cannot undo.

Moreover, in the last section of this chapter, I highlight the risk of romanticizing this transition and elevating it to an ethical model (as we can see in Husserl, 1988; Scheler, 1954; Levinas, 1969; Serban, 2024), as it generates expectations that might cause distress on the mother and the baby. Instead, I would propose "gossip" as an hermeneutic descriptive approach to better capture the nature of such a transformative event in the woman's life.

II. What Kind of Subject Is the Pregnant Mother?

Pregnancy represents a psychological and physical revolution in the woman's life. If until pregnancy certain gregariousness and camaraderie were shared between men and women, then the differences between the two sexes become increasingly dividing during pregnancy and motherhood.[2] Resentment often grows out of this isolating separation, as it seems that only the primary caregiver, often the woman, sees her life changing completely and her personal time shrinking. From there on, the woman's life takes a trajectory that is not comparable with her husband's, male friends' and colleagues'. In less than a year, her body progressively ceases to be fully hers in order to be at service of a new life that needs to be nurtured, sheltered and cherished until birth. As Marzia wrote,

"Pregnancy is physical. Motherhood starts before that. In pregnancy the body no longer belongs to you". What the woman has been in her life-world up to that moment can still continue to be, but she is standing on the precipice of a big unknown that will change her life.

Hence, in front of the untamable unknown, resentment grows. As this user writes[3]:

> Does anyone else feel burning resentment towards their partners? Just to be clear, I love my partner, he's a wonderful man and a great dad and I also obviously love my velcro LO with every inch of my being, I love bedsharing and contact napping and all that shizzle. BUT. BUT . . . sometimes I'm green with envy that my partner's life has seemingly barely changed.

Resentment might build up when realizing that only one life is going to dramatically change in this important transformation. Even if the partner can be very caring and mindful, sometimes they do not have the incarnated experience of what it feels like to be the main protagonist of this transition:

> Being a mom has been one of my greatest joys and deepest internal struggle.
> The day to day overwhelm, the expectation of being a loving nurturing mother and being boss, being a home maker, being available for every urge my partner has, being overly joyed that I have a partner who helps but doesn't do a full half of the work load.
> Sometimes I wonder if there is even a half it never ends?
> This morning as I cleaned up the kitchen and put my head phones on I listened to my dance music and danced a bit and a little grief layed over my heart.
> I miss you, I miss dancing. I miss the joy of feeling my beautiful spirit.
> I think my partner does too.
> I felt the urge to share to say out loud "I'm happy but I'm also miserable sometimes. I'm lonely but never alone".

Becoming a mother can be the fulfillment of one's life dreams and a deeply isolating experience—for both partners. No oxymoron keeps together the two sides of this coin; joy and sorrow are, in fact, two coexistent aspects of the same lived experience. How can philosophy help us describe the defining moments of transformation for women who deliver a baby, experience a stillbirth or go through a miscarriage? The woman becomes a pregnant woman and/or an expecting mother (in case of adoption or surrogate), then she decides whether to become a mother or any form of secondary caregiver, or just the person who gave birth to the baby. In all those cases, she will have to bid farewell to the person she used to be. As this woman writes "a little grief" came when she started dancing with her headphones on because for a brief moment she encountered "her beautiful spirit" and started wondering if she will ever encounter that spirit again.

II.1   Me, You and Our Bodies: Bodily Schemas

I believe it is important, if not finding a definite answer, at least to reflect on the questions around this transformation, since we all have been born from women who had to face some of these cogent interrogatives. The answers that the women of our lives found, whether on a conscious or unconscious level, shaped for a good part the persons we are today. We became *children of* these women or *children of* the interaffective community that was around us. Either way, that choice is what shaped our present. In fact, in pregnancy, as Merleau-Ponty remarks, "What happens in me can pass over into the other" (1995, p. 121). This capacity to experience the affect of others is magnified during infancy but nonetheless remains with us throughout our lives to varying degrees. When pregnant, the mother and her baby co-experience a number of affects that generate, through habitual repetitions, new corporeal schemas. The corporeal schema is the pre-reflective representation that we have of our body, and it is what allows our body to function in time and space according to a number of habits and repeated behaviors that we put into practice in our daily lives.

Independent of the ambivalence a mother is facing during pregnancy, a corporeal schema is nevertheless generated as an incarnated space of co-experience that deeply connects the two of them. When pregnant, the woman acquires new corporeal schemas that are deeply interconnected with the baby's schemas and mutually influenced. For example, she needs to get used to being thicker, to eat healthy and more, and to give up on certain daily chores. The baby, too, might tend to kick when the woman eats sugary food or stretch when listening to her humming a melody; ultimately, the baby too creates new corporeal schemas connected to his/her environment.

Far from being passive agents, both child and mother develop an interconnected identity that is strongly relational (Quintero & De Jaegher, 2020). Lymer (2011) proposes that mother and fetus entertain a bidirectional affective-communicative relationship. That is, affects impress both mother and fetus in the way in which they move and interact with each other in the world. A loud noise, for example, might scare the baby and her mother in their own ways. The mother's heart might accelerate and the baby's legs might start kicking; they might feel each other and have an additional reaction in feeling each other. Lymer connects maternal experience with empirical studies that show how fetal responses to maternal actions, like voice, touch (Marx & Nagy, 2015) and stress situations (DiPietro et al., 2013), can generate bodily schemas. In the constant reaction to each other and reactions to the outside world, a mother and her baby build a bond that creates a pattern of bodily habit that connects the two of them even before coming to life.

II.2   Phenomenological Views

The fascination generated by this complex form of interconnectedness led phenomenologists to reflect on the status of subjectivity that the woman holds during this time. As highlighted by Smith, Husserl's extensive writings on sexuality, womanhood, intrauterine life and birth prove his profound engagement with the philosophical implications of these phenomena, ultimately shaping the trajectory of transcendental phenomenology (Smith, 2016, p. 29).[4] In recent decades, the phenomenological discourse surrounding pregnancy has seen a notable proliferation, owing much to seminal works such as Young's renowned paper on "Pregnant Embodiment" (1984).[5] The body of the woman has been compared with a vessel (Neuhmann, 1955, p. 111) that carries the baby to its full development or with a fused entity in which it is not possible to distinguish the woman from her baby (Young, 1984).

In contrast with this view, I think that the woman's body is more than the instrument that carries this cluster of cells to a new life in the world because during this journey her body actually changes and engages with the new life from a pre-reflective to a reflective life. Hence, it would be wrong to compare the woman's body to a vessel because we would miss the transformative and interactive aspect of the embodied relationship that connects the woman with her baby. At the end of this journey, this "vessel" will never be the same as it was at its departure. Moreover, while Young refers to a split or a fusion between the two bodies, I believe that there is in fact a space of co-existence that is bodily created during pregnancy and somehow preserved throughout life.

While numerous scholars contend that when pregnancy is examined through phenomenological lenses, it challenges fundamental distinctions in Western philosophy, notably the subject-object dichotomy and the distinctions between self and other, and own and alien. I believe that the category that is challenged in pregnancy is the I-we because in pregnancy this category emerges as a primordial incarnated being. Hence, if Young (1984)[6] sees the woman fused with or even lost in the new life, she is carrying in herself, I see that the work that the woman is doing during this time is possibly even more complex. Young contends that the pregnant mother is unable to differentiate between herself and the infant, as well as between her own belongings and those of her child. According to her, this blending extends to both kinesthetic sensations of movement and ownership of body parts and physical spaces.[7] Different from this view, I believe that the woman is creating a new sensory-motor identity, or, to use a metaphor, the mold for an I-thou relationship that will model their long-lasting life in the life-world. A new body schema emerges from this experience that will shape their sensory-motor as well as emotional and interpersonal lives. As it is for surrogates or adopting mothers, she can still decide if that life will be or not under her care, but the incarnated process that leads to the constitution of this mold is irreversible and unstoppable.

Another phenomenological argument posits that the organic process of childbirth marks the initial experiential separation between self and other. According to this perspective, the relationship between mother and fetus does not involve interactions between two distinct corporeal selves, with such interactions emerging only after birth. This perspective has found support in the work of scholars such as Schües (1997, 2000) and Oksala (2003). Different from this, I believe that during this time we build that fundamental bridge that sustains the structure of intercorporeality and intersubjectivity so crucial for healthy psycho-physical functioning as human beings in our life-world. Kristeva, too, talks about the abyss that is between me and the child:

> [T]here is the abyss between the mother and the child. What connection is there between myself, or even more unassumingly between my body and this internal graft and fold, which, once the umbilical cord has been severed, is an inaccessible other? My body and . . . him. No connection.
>
> *(Kristeva, 1980, pp. 4)*

More than the abyss, I agree with Heinämaa when she writes:

> [T]he gestating woman is separating or divorcing from her earlier form of embodiment and at the same time establishing new boundaries for her own body. Rather than being characterized by loss of selfhood, pregnancy must be understood as a form of self-transformation.
>
> *(2014)*

The woman in the former excerpt, grieving for her beautiful spirit might receive some comfort in looking at herself as a transforming chrysalis. Her spirit will not be lost but transformed into something fitting her new being.

Therefore, to address the questions raised earlier, I believe that the gestating woman is creating a new sensory-motor identity, an I-we, that will accompany both the woman's and the baby's lives independent of the caring choice that the woman will make or the length of life that they will have together. In what follows, I will explain how this peculiar form of I-We is formed in the bodily schema.

III. How Do We Perceive the Other in Pregnancy? Double Intention

Phenomenology reinterprets Descartes' dualism by questioning not the existence of the other but rather how we perceive and engage with them. Husserl's way of questioning Descartes transforms his dualism into an incarnated process that helps us to see the other as a living, co-existent being sharing our life-world. The emphasis lies not on whether we can access the other but on the manner in which we perceive and interact with them. Consequently, from this point of view, being in the world manifests in the way with which we engage with the world through the empathetic connections we can establish with ourselves and the other.

While Young (1984) correctly emphasizes the role that double intentionality plays in pregnancy, I also believe that in pregnancy the I-we bond is established through the empathetic acts that operate in a peculiarly embodied way. According to Young, during pregnancy, the mother operates according to a double aim: one strives for the generation of the baby, the other is focused on completing small daily chores. This double intentionality brings this unique couple together in the accomplishment of double directed intentions. As Summa and colleagues (2022) elucidate, double intentionality often operates in emotionally complex lived experiences wherein our intent to do something overlaps with other acts such as remembering or expressing some feelings. One intention is directed at (*intentio recta*) intentional objects, and the other (*intention obliqua*) reflects on them (Brentano, 1995, pp. 78–79, 211–212), Hartmann (1985, pp. 46–47), Sowa (2007) and Moran (2013). The two do not need to be interlaced or to refer necessarily to the same objects. I can drive and meditate on what my father told me when I was at home, for instance. In pregnancy, the two ends of this double intention tend to often encounter each other and to generate an embodied intersubjective structure through empathetic acts.

It might be that driving is a moment for me to meditate on the events of the day, but it is improbable that every time I drive I meditate on what my father told me when we were in our kitchen at home. On the other hand, during pregnancy, double intentionality tends to repeat in related double acts in such a way that a habitual embodied pattern develops from this encounter toward interaffective habitual layers. In the long run, this creates the structure for a personhood that will accompany the mother and the baby until the next transformation.

For example, my habit of reflecting on things while driving in the car expresses a form of double intentionality where the two intentional acts tend to remain unrelated to each other, while my feeling the baby kick every time I am eating something sweet or listening to rock music are two related forms of *recta* and *obliqua intentio*. The repetition of these acts creates layers of sensory-motor experience, which will accompany the two living beings for a good part of their lives. My body will remember how the baby used to kick at a certain song, and the baby will feel soothed when hearing that song. That is why a miscarriage, for example might leave a sensory-motor schema that will influence the new pregnancy in the development of a new sensory-motor schema. The new pregnancy might be characterized by more anxiety in relation to certain actions or situations. Kicks—or the lack thereof—might not be lived as joyous encounters with the baby but as a reason to feel anxious and raise concerns about the newborn's well-being.

III.1 The Role of Empathy in Double Intentionality and the Sensory-Motor Identity

To show how a new sensory-motor identity and its related habits are generated from double intentionality, I need to briefly explain how empathy tends to unfold itself in this intentional activity. According to phenomenology, empathy is a form of perception that operates mostly through three steps: perceptive pairing, reflexive revelation and co-experiencing.

While in the first trimester for some women, pregnancy might not still be real, in the second semester, the baby becomes a real living being. As Jane recounts (cited in Bergum, 1986, p. 72), she was ambivalent about her pregnancy until the baby started kicking. When she felt her baby kicking, her ambivalence dissolved, and she dedicated herself to that new life with joy. From a phenomenological standpoint, those first kicks show the first encounter of the two ends of double intentionality into a form of perceptive pairing. The baby appears to be a living being in a way that is very similar to the mother's life. They both can kick. If until that moment the mother might have experienced difficulties in picturing the life of a dividing cell, with the kicks she realizes that a human life in all very similar to hers is touching her body. This perception pairs the two together. What was once a blastocyst, then an embryo, is now a fetus that has legs; with these legs, s/he is kicking the mother from within her own womb. This perception is a key moment to connect the two living beings and the two forms of intentions in an interaffective and intersubjective structure. The otherness of this life is given to the woman as a presence tied to the here and now of her body (Husserl, 1973, p. 99).

In this sense, empathy is first a mode of apperception and appresentation (Husserl, 1973, p. 229; Stein, 1970) that is founded on the concrete apperception of the living body or the material thing in front of me. It is a *Verbildlichung*: an act of analogizing or picture-making. This act occurs in a mutual way; we recognize each other as human beings living similar challenges (Scheler, 1954; Husserl, 2001; Gurwitsch, 1966). The subject gains initial access to the other's expressions, allowing them to perceive both the essence of life conveyed and the stylistic nuances embedded as referents shaping the subject's perception.

The second step of the empathetic connection involves reflexive revelation, that is, through the perception of the other, we learn something about ourselves. Carrying the pregnancy to term and giving birth to this baby (*directa intentio*) points to me at each moment something about myself (*obliqua intentio*). I notice myself becoming thicker, being unable to complete the smallest tasks I could thoughtlessly fulfill before; my clothes look funnier (at best). Or, to reflect on more meaningful aspects, I experience a sense of vulnerability I did not know before: my short breath reminds me that two hearts are beating in my body, and I feel invested by a sense of responsibility that I had not experienced before. The double intentions operating during and after pregnancy connect the two beings together through a reflexive revelation that strengthens the connection between the two bodies—independent of the result of the pregnancy or what the woman will decide to do with the care of her baby. In fact, I believe that even if the mother will give away the baby after birth and decide to not develop an emotional bond with them, a primal embodied empathetic connection is in any case there because the habitual encounters between the two lives occurred through double intentionality. These encounters contributed to cementing a primal interaffectivity that will shape both lives from there on.

As it concerns the second step, in perceiving the other, we feel our similarity and radical difference from one another in what we might call *reflexive revelation* or, to use Husserl's language pairing association (Husserl, 1970, 1973; Ricoeur, 1990). As Husserl remarks, the subject's perception of the other raises awareness of one's own life; in this perception, we become aware of the similarities and differences between ourselves and the other. While feeling closer to the other, we grow the sense of our undetermined understanding of the other's expressions. The subject relates to the other by shared life experiences perceived as akin. The resonance emanating from this pairing represents a passive synthesis of meaning that builds a connecting bond between individuals. Pairing aspects of each other's life involve a reflexive revelation (Husserl, 2001, p. 508; Ricoeur, 1990, p. 115) of the subject and the other according to particular profiles, characteristics and ties (Husserl, 1973, p. 114); the subject feels drawn to get attuned to those meanings of the other's expressive life that are personally salient for the subject as well.

While until this point the double intentionality of the woman and the baby tends to interconnect through a pre-reflective incarnated process, the last step of the empathetic unfolding requires a reflective choice. This third step involves, in fact, a co-experiencing and expanding of one's interaffective world into the world of the other according to one's own bodily will. In this step, in fact, we reflect on the meaning of the perceptive pairing and reflexive revelation, and we start co-habiting within each other's world. This is the step that maybe surrogates decide not to take. They will not take on the role of mothers and cohabit within the baby's world. In deciding to be in each other's world, despite the uniqueness of each one's traits, the similarities become affective anchors charged with emotions and resonant with one's own experience and the values they attach to it. Through these connecting points, new shared worlds and interaffective realities can be disclosed (Husserl, 1973; Schutz Fuchs/Koch). Interaffectivity is regarded as an intertwinement of two cycles of embodied affectivity in which continuously the two bodies resonate with each other and affect each other (Fuchs & Koch, 2014) through bodily and emotional interconnection (Zajonc, 1980; Hatfield et al., 1994). It is on this level that the woman attaches meanings and values to bodily schemas and affective responses she might experience in relation to her baby. These are the moments in which little habits, nesting activities, daydreaming or fears might arise as meaningful acts that will contribute to the constitution of a new foundational value system. Taking delight in the expressions the baby makes while breastfeeding, or taking pleasure from discovering the character that the baby reveals as they start growing contributes to the constitution of new bodily schemas in the mother and the baby. At this level, the woman does not need mental representations to feel what the baby is going through because there is a bodily resonance in action that instinctively connects them to each other (Merleau-Ponty, 1995). Those become activities that generate a certain value and meaning for them. For this reason, according to phenomenological and enactive approaches, human sociality does not start from isolated individuals and their hidden inner states but from interaffectivity (Husserl, 1973). We are embodied beings from the beginning. We can survive in this world because we participate in an embodied interaffectivity (with others), which gives us a sense of vitality that allows us to go through this life.

IV. Generative Stories

The empathetic bridge that is built between mother and child generates an embodied intersubjective structure that will shape the way in which we will live as human beings in this life-world. This bridge represents the basis of a "co-humanity", insofar as it expresses the original bonds of human togetherness (see Husserl, 1973, pp. 38, 393, and 584, Hua XV). As Husserl remarks, it represents that "'instinctive' relatedness to the world ('instinktive' Weltbezogenheit)", which begins in the mother's womb during prenatal life (Husserl, 2014, p. 222; Hua XLII, p. 10). An "instinctive relatedness to others (instinktive Bezogensein auf Andere)" that commands how "the beginning of our intersubjective life originates in the relation to the mother"[8] (Husserl, 2014, p. 461, Hua XLII). Through pregnancy, a new sensory-motor identity is created that will condition the development of both lives. As Heinamaa remarks, "Human persons, delineated by finitude and mortality, are also generative beings who are able to connect to one another across the boundaries of birth and death" (2020), and as Miglio continues, they are "embodied and relational from the very origin of their lives" (2019, p. 82). Their connection will become the bearer of future events and stories.

In this sense, the instinctive bond that connects both bodies in this original space of "co-humanity" needs to be respected as much as possible. Considerations of safety for the mother and/or the baby, for instance, frequently entail intruding interventions directed at the woman and the infant's corporeal entities, yet oftentimes without due regard for the instinctive bond linking the woman to her own physique and that of her offspring. It is crucial to always acknowledge whose body and whose baby are intimately involved in this singular, generative experience. I believe that women's bodies have the wisdom to deliver a baby and raise them. Regardless of the challenges at hand to understand this wisdom, it is necessary to give them the space to express their instinctive connection to their baby. As Odent (1981, p. 9) remarked decades ago, this point is still relevant today:

> These last years, we understand better and better what to do to help the mother become more instinctive, to forget what is cultural, to reduce the control of the neocortex, to change her level of consciousness so that the labour seems to be easier. For example, assistance by a female is always beneficial. . . . Women must engage themselves effectively to bring love, and at the same time to bring experience, as a mother would.

Among the activities that were in practice to facilitate women's delivery—that we hope we have now left behind—are the routine perineal shave and episiotomy, which we know today as pointless ways to expropriate the woman from the agency of her own parturition. These are among the many intrusive ways in which the embodied lives of the woman and her baby are not respected. According to Odent, we should adjust hospitals to women's instincts rather than expecting women to conform to hospital protocols.[9]

As recounted in the first chapter on the point:

> In 2022, on the second of the three days of labor to deliver my baby, a nurse came to my bed to convince me to insert a tube to check on the vitals of my baby. I could not move. I was attached to monitors and IV to receive antibiotics. I was an at risk pregnancy because of my age (42) and the time of labor was adding to it; so I asked the nurse if it was strictly necessary to insert this tube. After all, I was already connected to fetal monitoring during the whole labor to check on my baby's vitals. She said that it was not necessary but she was visibly concerned. Then the morning comes. I realize it only because a new shift starts and a new nurse comes. I was exhausted. My husband was asleep. The new nurse doesn't ask. She checks something on the monitor and she puts a tube inside me to further monitor my baby. Finally after 72 hours of labor I am ready to push. My baby comes out and his head is bleeding. My husband and I are worried, although overwhelmed by the joy of seeing him for the first time. My husband asks what that bleeding was. The nurses mutter some excuses. Two days afterwards, I was discharged without any official explanation. What they told me was that my ribs hurt my baby while in the womb, hence the bleeding. Of course, an external pediatrician at the first visit confirmed that the scar (which will remain for all his life and fortunately will not bring him any particular neurological harm as far as we know) was due to the tube they inserted.

In this story, the wish to do only what was strictly necessary was clearly expressed. She knew that her baby was asking for time to adjust, and she needed to be patient in her wait. She felt that things were going well, and she was up to taking full responsibility in case they were not. Yet she ended up taking responsibility for a practice that she ostensibly did not allow, the insertion of the tube, and she had to take the blame for a lie—her ribs supposedly hurt the skull of her baby. This story is similar to many others in which the mother-child bond was not respected.

Another lived experience that counterbalances this one is Anna's. They decided to have their baby at home. This decision brought them to the realization of the fragility of life. In choosing this option, they became completely aware of their full responsibility toward their baby's life. As her husband recounts, "we dehumanized death with hospitals because we delegated to the hospital, and its structure, the life and death of our loved ones" (cited in Bergum, 1986, p. 84). Whether we are at the hospital or at home, tragedy can happen. Brenda and her husband opted for a home birth for their child, thereby assuming accountability for any potential adverse outcome. In contrast, if complications were to arise in a hospital setting, it is common for the blame to be deflected onto the medical team, with expressions of sympathy for their efforts. However, should difficulties occur during a home birth, societal judgment often falls heavily on the parents, branding them as irresponsible or even attributing them with culpability for the outcome.

Women's bodies are inherently designed for childbirth and are capable of managing the process without the need for medical interventions enforced on them, such as episiotomies, enemas or heavy, unrequested medications. Whether we opt for hospital or at-home birth, we are undeniably the primary participants, or rather, as I endeavor to illustrate, the interrelated subjects of this intricate journey, and thus we bear responsibility for any unforeseen circumstances that may arise. When this autonomy is respected, the birthing process stands a greater chance of yielding positive outcomes without lingering negative effects.

A comparison between hospital and home births further illuminates this point. Christie succinctly encapsulates her hospital birth experience with the phrase "they did a lot to me" (cited in Bergum, 1986, p. 157), with the doctor even asserting "don't do that to me again" as if he were the central figure in the event. She recounts how hard and traumatizing her birthing process was. She was not allowed to squat or find a position that would have helped her to push. She remembers having received drugs she was not aware of that led her to lose control over her body. She felt scared, and apparently her doctor, too, felt under pressure in such a situation. This stands in stark contrast to Anna's narrative, summarized by the phrase "we did it ourselves". Anna delivered at home. She and her husband recount the respectful and unobtrusive presence of the midwives throughout the process. "They didn't intervene much during labor . . . there was a sense of harmony in their collaborative approach" (cited in Bergum, 1986, p. 157). Often, being there as a respectful presence for the women can help to overcome the challenges of a normal delivery. Adjusting to the woman's needs can facilitate the expression of that intersubjective embodied bond that is cemented during pregnancy.

V. What Are the Transformative Moments in Pregnancy and Early Motherhood?

What are the transformative moments that characterize this transition? How do we change? As mentioned earlier, we know that we do not change overnight. Parenthood starts before getting pregnant. As Elliott wrote, "No one just woke up pregnant one day. As a gay man, the journey to parenthood was expensive, socially challenging, legally perilous, and often very lonely". Is it possible to say no to the magnitude of this change? In what follows, I mark out some of the transformative moments of this complex journey.

V.1 Self-Transformation and Teleology

Transhumanists consider that the main trait of human essence is a pursuit of self-transcendence, synonymous with advancing freedom or autonomy, aiming to surpass all limitations posed by "natural" and biological constraints. As Simone de Beauvoir rightly points out, the form of transcendence that invests the woman and her baby is different from the self-transcendence that human beings normally live in their lives. For example, the craft person might experience a sense of self-transcendence when they apply their talent and manage to create something unique. In that sense, the experience of transcending is in fact *trans*, beyond, the limits of their own biological body because it concretizes itself in the object created. In the transition from pregnancy to motherhood, the woman transcends her own biological limits in an immanent way by remaining in her own body. Beauvoir contends that the conventional Hegelian-Sartrean framework, which depicts the self and the other engaged in a confrontational struggle for acknowledgment, is, in this generative case, called into question. Pregnancy experiences challenge this model by presenting a scenario where two sensory-motor entities exist in a relationship devoid of conflict or mutual validation. As she writes:

> A new existent is going to manifest and justify itself, and she is proud of it. But she also feels herself moved by obscure forces, tossed and violated. What is specific to the pregnant woman is that the body is experienced as immanent at the moment when it transcends itself. . . . The transcendence of the artisan, of the man of action is inhabited by one subjectivity, but in the becoming mother the opposition between subject and object is abolished. She forms with this child from which she is swollen an equivocal couple overwhelmed by life.
>
> *(Beauvoir, 1987, p. 512)*

Obscure forces move the woman from within; she overcomes herself within herself without challenging the otherness but making the otherness part of her very own essence. The new-existent becomes a co-existent that is molded within her, which not even death can undo. A new structure of intersubjectivity that was embedded in her body becomes manifest in this primordial intercorporeal structure. The teleological predisposition that was silent in the woman becomes active and operates from within the woman, like "obscure forces that violate and toss her". The woman already has inside herself the norm for this new intersubjective mold, despite the discomfort it might entail. Biological processes such as menstruation, lactation, breast swelling and belly expansion entail discomfort and pain. However, contrary to being perceived as abnormal, they contribute to defining a new norm for the female body. While these occurrences deviate from women's daily bodily processes, they establish a normative framework. Pregnancy involves a teleological predisposition in women to bear a child that nevertheless leads to a sense of bodily estrangement. The body is inherently prepared for this condition, with its ordinary functions facilitating the accommodation of another living being. During pregnancy, the internal body ceases to be a vague mass and instead becomes a defined space for another entity. These functions are inherent to the individual, involving the sensing and movement of another being.

The transcendent effort of creating a "Mitsein" (in-between world) within oneself as a fundamental aspect of human experience represents the inherent interconnectedness among individuals rather than a separate entity. When a woman becomes pregnant, the concreteness of her living present takes a new form according to the teleology of her body. There seems to occur an expropriation of time as uniquely her own. The living present of her *substratum,* the original flow or the light through which what comes to evidence is luminous (Hua XIV, 45, 301) shows an I-we that was not present before. This form of time constitutes the core for immanent concrete time[10] that we recognize when we organize it in the mundane form of a chain of before-afters. Despite always being there, the intersubjective being of the concreteness of her body stands out in her present moment. This new form of time requires a reorganization that is difficult to translate into words, values and actions.

The form in which the woman used to express herself before is obsolete since she is now expressing her teleology into an I-we. The obscure forces Beauvoir referred to that toss and violate her from within are expressed by this teleological movement that becomes evident to us through time. According to Husserl, teleology "is the latest for us and the first in itself. Why? It must be the totality as totality already disclosed in its whole system of particular forms" (Ms E III, 9). The teleological final form is the latest for us to see because we are capable of perceiving the form of chaotic matter and recognizing its value only at the very end of its unfolding process; yet it is the first in itself because without this unfolding nothing would be given to us. In what follows, I emphasize some of the elements of the chaotic change that contribute to the transformative process endured by the woman's identity.

Pain

Pain constitutes a significant component of a woman's transition to motherhood, whether it manifests physically or emotionally. It appears to be a pervasive element intertwined with the experience of maternal initiation. As Kana and Maren tell us, pain seems to be an inevitable step in the process of becoming a mother:

> Pain was among my imagination. Although I had a big fear before the birth of my daughter, after my daughter was born, my love for her just flooded like a fountain.
>
> The fear of being pregnant and giving birth, the changes my body will undergo, the development of another body in me, the responsibility that comes with it, the pain and total loss of control.

Pain is part of the process and should be neither idealized nor perceived as punitive toward the parturient woman, despite the etymological association of the term "pain" with the Latin word "poena", signifying punishment. Romance languages such as Italian do not employ, in fact, this Latin root to denote women's suffering; rather, emphasis is placed on the passive aspect of pain through the term "suffering" (*sub-fero*, to tolerate). The pain inherent in the birthing process need not be construed as the biblical decree of punishment upon women or passively accepted as an inevitable precursor to the commencement of new life. Indeed, enduring the pain of childbirth represents a pivotal moment in the transformative journey of a woman into motherhood. Through this process, the woman engenders both her child and her own identity as a mother. Pain emerges as a meaningful element that accompanies the revelation of truth in this profound experience. As these testimonies show:

> On paper, I had an ideal "natural" (except the induction of course) and gave birth to a healthy child after 12 hours, no complications, not even stitches needed. I entered the hospital at 7am and left the same day shortly before midnight with my partner and baby (also because they needed the bed of course, and I was able to somehow move). Still, this was a limit experience, with immense pain and feelings of anxiety and complete helplessness. For most women birth is traumatic, due to complications, pain, but also the circumstances, that is, how you are treated in hospital.
>
> First of all, the whole thing is not about you, your pain, body or state of mind is not as important, your body is in the service of giving birth, the main medical goal is to guarantee the survival and successful birth of the child (which includes your well-being to a certain extent of course). (Maren)

> Does the pain of labour have any value—she wondered. And I learned about myself. I loved my husband even more. I look back at myself and I can't believe how I used to be.
>
> *(cited in Bergum, 1986)*

Pain is such a pervasive element that seems to have its function in the transformation of the woman into a mother:

> In pain, there is an experience of being inward and involved in feeling the pain not enjoying it, but taking note, and enduring or whatever you do to handle it and knowing that it is going to produce a child. That is what it is not to focus on the pain but to see what the pain does to you and how it changes you.
>
> *(cited in Bergum, 1986)*

It entails a transcending movement because it forces the individual to focus on something that transcends the pain itself in order to make it manageable. Pain aims at the telos of its resolution; here, for example:

> I withdrew into myself, had a few thoughts. I was immersed in a physical sensation, with lack of awareness of time, or what was going on around me. I tried to find a comfortable position, was impatient, angry, and shaking. I feared that I wouldn't be able to stand the pain, which would be to lose myself and maybe even die. I screamed, or wanted to scream, to bite on something, I cried because it hurt so much. I didn't know what to do and needed someone to help me. I was brought to the core of myself, pitted against myself.
>
> *(cited in Bergum, 1986, p. 180)*

Time disappears. Not being able to stand the pain would mean to lose oneself and even die because everything becomes pain and we are swallowed by it. That is why, in pain, women transcend themselves and find themselves in a more real way.

In that sense, pain becomes the final telos of a transformative experience. It comes and goes in waves. This pain has a rhythm that gives origin to the most miraculous of the events, the birth of the new baby. Even the word birth comes from *Bara* (bore), which means wave. Birth itself, from its roots, comes from these waves of pain. "To bear children" originates from the root bãra in Old Norse, signifying wave, billow or bore. This linguistic connection emphasizes the metaphorical association of childbirth with waves, particularly in describing the contractions experienced during labor. Analogous to waves propelled by the tide, each contraction carries the baby closer to the mother's embrace. However, the wave analogy extends beyond mere description; it encapsulates various facets of the birthing process. Just as ocean waves vary in intensity and impact, the experience of labor encompasses sensations of being carried, caught or overwhelmed by the pain. The peak of discomfort occurs when the baby progresses through the narrow passage of the birth canal, akin to colliding tidal currents in an estuary. This metamorphic portrayal delineates the cyclical nature of pain during childbirth, from its onset and crescendo to eventual relief and preparation for subsequent waves of pain.

> Too tired to say anything, I push with all my might. I'm the Lilliputian. I may not be able to do it. It's beyond me to give birth to you.
>
> *(Chesler, 1979, p. 115)*

The pain of the vaginal birth or the pain of the C-section (often accompanied by a sense of guilt and powerlessness) represents ground steps for the epiphany of a meaning that would be constitutive of the new woman's identity and the being in the world of the new baby—a birth day in fact for both of them. As Chesler writes in her book With Child (1979):

> Last year, I died. My life without you ended. Our life together—only nine months!—ended too, abruptly and forever when you gave birth to me. Being born into motherhood is the sharpest pain I've ever known. I'm a newborn mother, your age exactly one year old today.
>
> *(1979, p. 281)*

As already mentioned in Chapter 1, preparing for motherhood requires the woman to face and accept death. It forces the woman to think about death. Pregnancy is still today a life-threatening event for the woman and her baby. Even if literal death does not occur, a metaphorical death touches the woman's previous personal identity; something major in her has to die to give way to a radical transformation. As in this last excerpt:

> Oh yes, we are finding furniture for the baby, preparing, getting ready . . . and there is preparation for death too. Are they really so different?
>
> *(Woodman, 1985, p. 140)*

As we prepare for a child in our life, we are forced to imagine the death of our child. We are forced to face our own mortality. As we begin to acknowledge our own death, our thoughts come back to the child for whom we are responsible (Oakley, 1980, p. 27). Becoming pregnant puts the woman in conversation with death.

Blood

Blood is another unequivocal sign of the woman's embodied life transcending into motherhood. The rhythm paced by the menstrual blood becomes a constant reminder of a possibility. As reported by a woman narrating her story, "Blood is the sign of hope and nothing done" (cited in Neuhmann, 74, 1955).

It was Catherine who said "that each moment her menstrual period demonstrated to her that nothing had been done about her decision to have a baby. The monthly rhythm of the female body, her woman's body, her bleeding reminded her that time was passing" (cited in Bergum, 1986, p. 74). Susan, too, was constantly thinking, maybe this month (Bergum, 1986).

The rhythm of women's bodies forces women to reflect on time in a phenomenological way. A bodily sign such as blood becomes the token of a time that does not simply indicate a before and after but phenomenologically reveals the meaning attached to an ever-present moment. The living present becomes a wonder about *the right* time for having children. As Kana shares with us:

> I had a natural desire to be a mother, maybe it came from my instinct, or it was an intention of the society where I belonged to, to educate girls to think like that. Anyway, I had a dream to be a mother. When I was small, I thought about how my children would look like, how they would be called, and so on. . . . the fact that I have endometriosis, which is known to be related to infertility, the inner me tried to hurry up and think about having children in the not far future.

Motherhood starts before the actual pregnancy when we look at that monthly blood and time becomes ripe for a meaningful decision. That blood forces the woman to attend to the question of the right time and embrace her self-transcending transformation, whether it ends in a pregnancy or in the decision of remaining without children.

For example, blood marks are also the sign of miscarriages or alert signs during pregnancy. Being able to coexist with little drops of blood during pregnancy requires quite a challenging exercise. Even actions as simple as going to the bathroom become an intense trigger because the woman is at each time confronted with the possibility of finding new drops of blood and made her to confront with her sense of vulnerability. Not to mention the amount of blood a woman has to experience during a miscarriage when it becomes highly possible that those so potentially precious cells will be flushed down the toilet during the days of miscarriage. As narrated in this excerpt:

> I also remember the sense of hopelessness, fear, and vulnerability I experienced at my first miscarriage. The doctor asked me to wait for the body to spontaneously expel "the material" (that material already had a name for me, so much I had desired to get pregnant before). After 10 obnoxious days in which I had to learn how to walk around the world with this now dead life inside of me, which just a few days before was the promise of new dreams and

projects, she gave me pills that would have facilitated its expulsion. The language gap made everything more uncertain; she was speaking German while my first language was Italian. I was not sure I understood all that there was to do. I remember I came back home taking these pills and started cramping alone on my couch. After a few hours of contractions—to my expense, I discovered that not only birthing women experience contractions but miscarrying ones, too—the blood started coming. Plenty of blood. In my ingenuity I had bought for myself a package of chips and another package of chocolate chip cookies thinking that that was all tI needed. Little I knew that the affair of miscarrying a fetus was a much more serious deal. Nobody prepared me for what I faced. I was carrying myself from the couch to the bathroom. Flushing the toilet with bloody material of the baby I desired to have for all my life; it was psychologically devastating but even more was the pain. . . . In the end, my sister's call saved me. She was in Italy, I was in Switzerland. By that time I had lost quite an amount of blood. She asked me how many pills I had already taken. I told her that I was not sure if I should keep taking those pills at the same rate as my doctor suggested. She encouraged me to call the doctor again to check. It was impossible to get her on the phone. Eventually I ended up calling an emergency doctor. Everyone is talking in German I barely understand. Finally a woman understood I was Italian. She guides me step by step about what to do. After a few hours the blood quiets down and so do the cramps. I managed to fall asleep. For all that time it did not cross my mind for even one second to call for help. My sister called just out of personal care. In the evening my husband arrived and saw me just a little more tired than usual. That blood was mine. That moment of desperation and pain was supposed to be all mine. That day I became a mother, even though it was just blood and empty dreams. Probably I wanted to be alone. I did not know how to let anyone else enter in that complicated psychological and physical space. Before that, I thought of miscarriages as little moments of illness comparable to a fever or a flu. My mother had some but I never fully understood.

As this story shows, learning how to cope with blood is a transformative experience that confronts women with one of their biological teloi from an early age. That blood marks a separating line between men and women.

Trusting the Body: Divinity and Vulnerability

The transition from pregnancy to early motherhood represents an important transformation for the woman's body. The usual clothes will no longer fit. The shape of her body will strongly change, and in some cases it will not come to its original shape (breast, chest, maybe belly may take a new shape). It will be difficult for the woman to feel at ease in the new shape and to recognize herself in the mirror. The body might become a foreign entity that is difficult to trust and accept, even in the smallest daily activities. As Brenda recounts:

> I find my body really hard to accept. You understand that this is a baby growing inside of you and you have to get bigger and you see your body growing different and there are deposits of fat and stuff. It is ok so far it is hard, it's firm, but you know that it will be jelly like later on. It is hard to accept. I step on the scales and they say I weigh that much. I believe that you can have a child and you can go back down to 115 pounds afterwards there is no reason why you shouldn't. I feel that there should be the way it was before. We saw a film about the natural child and cesarean section at the prenatal class. I kept my eyes closed. Tom my husband was really impressed. Now he wants me to have a C-section. He says it's more humane, like he doesn't like to see a woman suffer he figures it would be less pain.
>
> *(cited in Bergum, 1986, p. 70)*

Trusting a birthing body is hard. Brenda's husband would prefer her wife (if not all women) to have a C-section rather than to endure all that pain with their bodies (as if a C-section would guarantee less pain). The miracle of birth is so impressive that one might wonder if this body can cope with such an enormous task. There are fears about being able to coexist with the damages that the birth will bring to the body: "Will my body come back as it used to"? (Brenda asks herself) or Camilla still feels unease toward the scar left by an unplanned C-section "In addition, I had an unplanned cesarean section, which greatly destabilized me because of the scar it left, which I still struggle to see as something positive". Brenda continues: "Even if I like myself now because there is a life inside me will I like myself later? The body becomes hard to accept and to trust". In this other testimony, Susan's story points out to her personal challenge in relation to her body: "I wanted people to know that I am pregnant and not fat" (cited in Bergum, 1986, p. 72). The insecurity she experienced was particularly evident when dancing for fun in a club or when obliged to face the scrutiny of her first-grade students who speculated about her weight gain.

The body becomes the terminus ad quem the woman has to relate. Before accepting the new life, she needs to accept this new body that will sustain her and her child for the months to come. It is not easy given the profound transformation it encounters before and after the pregnancy.

Susan, for example, recounts that despite her deep desire for motherhood, the disappointment of recurrent menstrual cycles left her weary of hope. However, upon discovering her pregnancy, she found a glimmer of faith in her body's capabilities once again. Ironically, it was during the process of pursuing adoption paperwork that Susan unexpectedly learned of her pregnancy through a routine medical examination. As her pregnancy progressed, her vulnerability heightened, exacerbated by concerns about the quality of medical care she might receive. Fearing the possibility of a harsh episiotomy at the hands of a doctor reputedly associated with more aggressive practices, Susan grappled with anxiety. Further moments of heightened vulnerability emerged when her husband was away skiing, as she fretted over potential accidents and the absence of his support. As the anticipated arrival of her baby approached, expectations clashed with reality when the birthing process did not unfold as swiftly as anticipated. The necessity for forceps intervention due to cervical retraction showed her the unpredictable nature of childbirth. Indeed, as Susan navigated the final stages of pregnancy, she experienced a profound sense of surrender as her body prepared for birth, echoing the sentiment articulated by Chesler (1979): "There's a moment in which the woman is too big. That's the time in which Nature helps the woman to get ready for the birth. It feels that the woman no longer holds her body" (65).

This feeling of surrender to the wisdom of the body and its vulnerability is mirrored by Christine's testimony (cited in Bergum, 1986, p. 82):

> I have felt more dependent than I've ever felt in my life. I feel physically vulnerable, that is, if I am with a bunch of people in a crowd, I could easily be thrown off balance. Through the winter, especially when I am driving the car, I don't want these crazy drivers coming near me. It is just that there is a baby here. Just lately in the last three weeks I feel careful about what I lift and haul and carry. Before it would be hard for me to let someone else do it. I mean, I'm very strong, and feel very strong and very capable and I can do this.

Carrying a baby in your body changes the connection one feels with one's own body and the way in which we can relate to it. A woman's body becomes strong and vulnerable; it has the power to generate life, but at the same time it needs to protect this life with each of its fibers. Moreover, after the baby is born, that exhausted body becomes the main source of sustenance for her baby and her own life. It is easy for mothers to question themselves and feel unsure about the rightness of their doing, especially in front of all the unknown that their bodies reveal to them. As mentioned in Chapter 4, it is the unknown itself that slowly shows its face and unveils the transformation:

> It was indeed a transformation for me. I was interested in those things that seemed so common (the inwardness one feels during labor), and how we differed (how we felt about our changing bodies). There is a great strength derived from birthing and mothering and I think it is an untapped resource.
>
> *(cited in Bergum, 1986, p. 64)*

The unknown that the woman progressively unveils during this transformation becomes an untapped resource of strength. Even though it might be obvious to emphasize the insecurities and vulnerability that women feel in relation to their bodies in that moment, it is key to acknowledge the sense of divinity enclosed in these transcending moments. Neuhmann, for example refers to the breastfeeding woman as the goddess cow (Neuhmann, 1955, p. 70), in contrast with another testimony of a woman who recounted how her pediatrician exclaimed to her, "[Y]ou're quite a cow!" because she was still breastfeeding her 12-month-old baby.

The Erosion of Time

Phenomenology stresses at least two notions of time, the phenomenological and the phenomenic one (more on this in Chapter 7). While this latter can be comparable to the linear sense of time, the former is a form of reflection that bears meanings and values that we attach to what each moment represents for us. In the transition from pregnancy to motherhood, time is a key element, especially in relation to the body. During labor, time becomes an eternal instant whose usual borders are eroded and its being comes to acquire a new shape. During labor, the light changes on the wall, and the clock seems to mark different moments in space, but the woman does not seem to feel the passing of this linear time. In front of her, there is a new living present that is different from all the other moments in which she attended to her present being. As this testimony recounts, the woman is inwardly completely focused on her body:

> I was in my body. . . . I was somewhere on the ceiling, alto breach, out of hearing. My thoughts were in one place, my body in another.
>
> *(Chesler, 1979, p. 255)*

After the baby's arrival, life becomes a flow divided into sections organized around the new life. As the words show:

> I think I am still organized and I think about things ahead of time. When I start making dinner, it is two in the afternoon, when I settle down because I know that till supper time is up. I just take advantage of the time I have.
>
> *(cited in Bergum, 1986, p. 70)*

Or the time we want to dedicate to romance and sex with our partner is no longer a spontaneous time of enjoyment. It is again a parcel of linear time dedicated to a specific purpose:

> If you want to have sex, we have to do it now because it is 20 to 10 and the babies are asleep. Whenever it happened to spontaneous love making.
>
> *(Kristin cited in Bergum, 1986, p. 85)*

As this Kristin remarks, having a child changes our sense of time. The phenomenological sense of time, that is the living present that connects past and future, shrinks in Leistungen, in functioning moments apt to the execution of specific purposes:

> Living with a child changes one's relationship to time. Instead of our 10 minutes, work time, coffee time or dinner time, etc. the days are broken into sleep time, feeding time, bathing time and laundry time. It might seem endless and one wonders if one can live through it. There is never enough time for sleep. There is not much time for oneself as a mother.

The phenomenological notion of time, that is the meaning we assign at each moment, changes once we have a baby or during their delivery is completely different and certainly diverges from the linear time as perceived by anyone else. Unless one spends time with a group of parents, it becomes difficult for others to see the pressing clock that ticks inside a mother's body. As recounted in the first chapter by Patricia:

> I would spend my days walking with her and friends who had infants, going to mommy and me groups or Gymboree or music classes and do my work when the nanny came. Sex was planned, if it happened at all, during her naps and once in awhile we would go on date night. Everything was scheduled in little boxes of time between her naps and feedings and the nanny and work. Nothing spontaneous at all and it all functioned best if I just accommodated everyone's needs. We didn't have a ton of money and the grandparents were either too old or too far away to be much help. If I wanted to sleep in or eat late or not stop at the park or talk for awhile with a friend or whatever, I would be penalized by crying and whining, which was hard to tolerate.

Nothing spontaneous. Everything must be planned to accommodate everyone's needs. As soon as a woman leaves her child to daycare, the babysitter or even if she still is with her child (because she knows, their patience will soon wear out), her clock is ticking, and every minute she is giving to someone else is extremely precious because these are minutes that she is not conceding to herself or to the long list of chores she has to complete.

Time and Exhaustion

According to this new perspective, the primary caregiver, in this case the mother, seems, to use Heideggerian terms, to have been thrown again in the world (1996). From here, she can choose whether to look at what this thrownness teaches her or not. Becoming a mother is an opportunity to renew her sense of time as she used to know it and follow a transcendental constitution of being according to the new rhythm that the intersubjective co-existence of the two lives will bring to the fore. As this new mother writes:

> I never understood what it meant for a day to have 24 hours until I had a child. Before Sasha, time was split into day and night. It was light, and then it was dark. It was time for sleep, then time to wake up. My calendar told me when I needed to be somewhere. My life was ruled by the clock. After the birth, time ceased to make sense in the way I'd understood it for most of my life. . . . In this new reality, timing was important, but time itself was meaningless.[11]

When navigating a new motherhood, time becomes a constitutive function that discloses to us our new intersubjective space. If during labor and in the few weeks afterwards we join the timelessness of time, after that a rhythm starts picking up from the depths of our organic being. It is from the pulsation of life that this rhythm shows us how our body, habits and social connections changed through this brief time, and every bit of information we gather in this rhythm brings us a meaning and a value that will help us to make sense of the radical changes that invested our lives. As Maren wrote:

> Suddenly you are being alone at home with baby you hardly know, on service 24hours a day, anxious and insecure most of the time, unable to take a break or sleep properly. Of course, there is this immense love for the little one that fills you, but mostly this love was experienced by me as concern. Every time she cried, my whole body was shaking, I was alert (will she cry or not) all the time. 6 weeks after birth, I went with little Emma for the first time for a walk in the stroller to my last appointment with the midwife. I was so tensed, alert, and anxious that she would begin to cry again (what they do when they are not used to being ride around with a stroller) that lost my way, came late, covered in sweat, and felt exhausted. In retrospect I cannot imagine why this was so difficult or why I was so anxious or tensed, as you get used to the crying and are able to anticipate the behavior of your little one, you know when it is serious and when it is just a crying hour. This continuous tension and alertness were unbearable, I felt as if I was going to get crazy or psychotic.

As the studies show, even if women regain some sleep and some time for themselves in the 24 months after the birth of their children, they might still feel exhausted and incapable of gathering the sufficient energy for a fulfilling life (Alsén et al., 2020). That might happen also because an inadequate constitution of meanings and values followed these months. The rhythmic time that pulsed into the new life to show the woman whom she became according to that intersubjective revolution that invested her failed to shed light on new layers of her being. When the person, the family or the social network around the woman does not support the transformation but somehow gives feedback of an image that is still anchored to the ways in which that person was before the intersubjective transformation, then it becomes problematic to recover from exhaustion. She is trapped in an existence and an ontological presence that do not reflect her actual life. The transformation that exhaustion brings to the fore often begins subtly, without our conscious awareness. Slowly but surely, we withdraw from activities we once enjoyed, avoid social interactions and become increasingly irritable. It is as if our very identity is overshadowed by fatigue, rendering us unrecognizable even to ourselves.

For example, expressions like "before you cared about my job, now you barely listen to me" might lead the woman to feel some guilt for not being able to welcome the affective information of people around her. The intersubjective nature of her new being might be overwhelming, and it might be possible that suddenly there is less space for her own thoughts, even less for job transitions of people around her. Being able to acknowledge that and see what might become habitualized and transformed into a new layer of identity can inform a positive transformation. From there, she might be able to educate her husband as to when she can be receptive to new sensitive information and maybe to increase her receptivity in certain moments. In return, she will feel more present and closer to herself.

If the woman does not get a chance to feel present to herself, she will not be able to be there for herself and the unfolding of her own story. What she lived would not acquire any particular sense. Following Merleau-Ponty's (1995) and Sartre's (1986) interpretation of exhaustion, she might be unable to follow the operative intentionality of her body and eventually feel tempted to withdraw from it as a weight that is impinging on her.[12]

Without the acceptance of what time is holding and presenting to her reflection, everything will be felt as an urgent moment of functioning that remains disconnected from the rest and cannot find a place in the story of her life. As I will describe more in Chapter 7, the woman needs to come out of the instantaneity of the event in order to see herself stretching in time, no matter how restricted this stretch might be. Being able to find her present would help her to find her presence in the new intersubjective being she re-presents.

VI. More Gossip, Less Ethics

As a closing remark, I would like to stress the importance of refraining from imposing or deducing the paradigm for any ethical structure from this complex lived experience. Using this embodied bond as a model for an ethical behavior might add more pressure on the complexity of this experience, spoiling the genuinity of the emerging sensory-motor identity between the two. In phenomenology, there are several examples of how this bond has been taken as a paradigm for the way humans should behave. I believe that romanticizing this fact of nature would enhance the problem of performative gender (Butler, 1988) and conforming to norms that are unfit for our personal growth.

Husserl presents the love that a mother has for her child as an ought of love as an example of the form of absolute love that characterizes value-feeling, different from impersonal values. According to Husserl, the love that a mother experiences for a child cannot be compared to the love that one experiences for a piece of classical music. When a mother has to make decisions about the well-being of her child, the absolute value of love prevails over any other rational value. In that sense, Serban (2024) fosters the view of this ought as a paradigmatic form of ethical behavior that is respectful of other human beings in the world. Although reasonable, I believe that said ethical strategy would further the harm that women have to bear when transitioning to the new maternal role. See, for example, Camilla's testimony:

> It may sound harsh, but I've come to realize that I'm not the kind of mom who would stay with her daughter 24/7 because I'd probably end up exhausted. I need the time spent with her to be quality rather than quantity, giving myself the necessary space to recharge each time. This is really important to me, and I believe my daughter will understand it too!

There are women who might find a piece of classical music as a better choice over taking care of the well-being of their child. They might delegate this act of care to the father while trying to find some respite from their maternal duties; yet, given the expectations pressing on them, they might also have to deal with the sense of guilt emerging from it.

Lévinas' phenomenological examinations of pregnancy, too, depict motherhood and parenthood as an ethical occurrence, unveiling a profound ethical foundation concerning the other and alterity (Morny, 1994; Katz, 2004). Lévinas posits that maternity epitomizes a profound responsibility toward others that arrives at substituting and enduring suffering on behalf of others. For the philosopher, parenting a new life shows an inherent ethical significance, wherein the maternal role entails assuming responsibility not only for those being cared for but also for those who inflict harm upon them. Similarly in Scheler, the loved one represents a spatial, corporeal (körperlich-räumlich) "part" of the one who loves (Scheler, 1973a, *Gesammelte Werke, Band VII (GW 7)*, Francke Verlag). In spite of Scheler's distinct contention that "the mother's identification with her child" occurs "in the maternal and parental instinct, not in motherlove" (Scheler, 1973a, p. 84, GW 7; Scheler, 2008, p. 73), for him, mothers and not fathers have the primordial instincts to truly love the other.

While I believe that women are capable of truly loving their children and, in contrast with Scheler, I believe that fathers are capable of this love as well, we still need to give them the space for misbehaving or just for taking some distance from their babies when they need it. We need to make space for bad mothers so that any mother, even when bad, can still remain a mother. Becoming a mother does not mean to become a saint or an ethical guide. For these reasons, I believe that motherhood cannot automatically stand as an ethical model of what one ought to do.

In that sense, I found fascinating the etymology of the word gossip. We might need to look at the experience of becoming a mother more as gossip than as an ethical paradigm. The term "gossip" originally referred to a child's godparent, who attended the birth ceremony out of concern for the child's present and future. Over time, the term evolved from "god-sib" to "gossip", specifically denoting female friends invited to be present at births in the sixteenth century. The informal conversations exchanged by these women during childbirth came to be known as gossip, representing a distinct form of discourse reflecting women's experiences and lives. As a discourse predominantly among women, gossip served as an alternative communication system, offering a space for intimate and trusted relationships. This chatter functioned as a ritualistic accompaniment to childbirth, symbolizing the ushering in of new life. The act of gathering to gossip symbolized the formation of friendships and mutual support, with the shared discourse contributing to the creation of a shared world (Grumet, 1983).

In routine conversation, speakers exhibit intricate interpretations of their experiences, which are further contextualized by the world around them. This context, characterized by its breadth, richness, fullness and unpredictability, shapes and enriches their discourse. As individuals uphold their personal mutable narratives and interests, the public dimension of women's private lives becomes apparent. The nuanced interpretation of routine conversation offered here enhances our understanding of women's transcending transformation, demonstrating a deep engagement with its complexities.

Being able to commit to the private and public story of someone and bring this to life is the best service we can do to understand the deeply transformative experience of becoming a mother.

VII. Conclusion

In this chapter, I reflected on the process of transformation that invests women in the transition from pregnancy to motherhood. One emerging element is that the transformation finds its roots even before pregnancy. For example, given the embodied and instinctive nature of this transition, the monthly period is already a bodily reminder for a decision that needs to be taken.

Moreover, once pregnant, the woman becomes the primal space for a form of embodied intersubjectivity that is strengthened by a double form of intentionality and a unique quality of empathetic acts. Questioning other phenomenological views, I argue that the woman does not lose herself in the fusion with the baby, but aiming at the creation of this new life, she is constantly reminded of its uniqueness by very embodied acts, such as kicks, stretches or hiccups. Her main intention of creating life connects with daily intentions, such as eating or working, ultimately resulting in the constitution of a bodily schema for her and her baby. In this way, the perceptive pairing that empathetically connects mother and baby cements a daily interconnection that builds the space for an interaffective and intersubjective being. This primordial space shapes the form of intersubjective connection we carry on throughout our lives as *children of* our caring adults.

In the second part of the chapter, I reflected on the steps that make the transformation possible, and I highlighted how the transformation has the quality of an immanent self-transcendence where the woman overcomes her limits while staying within her limits. The baby is her flesh and beyond her flesh. Using excerpts from various participants, I focused on some of the main steps through which the self-transcendence occurs, namely through the witnessing of the blood, enduring pain, trusting one's own growing body and connecting to time in a new way. As a concluding remark, I emphasized how a hermeneutic phenomenological approach should be favored to describe such a complex experience rather than an ethical one that elevates this living transformation to an ethical paradigm of behaviors.

Notes

1 The quote "We're born alone, we live alone, we die alone. Only through our love and friendship can we create the illusion for the moment that we're not alone" is widely attributed to Orson Welles. However, there is no confirmed source, such as a specific film or interview, directly linking this quote to Welles. It appears to be one of those quotes commonly associated with him but whose exact origin is unclear. Some speculate that it may have been said during one of his interviews or reflections, but it has not been traced to a verifiable source within his body of work.
2 For this point in transgender and homosexual couples living through this transition, see, for example, Tordoff et al. (2023).
3 In this chapter, when I employ the term user, I refer to forums that are hosted on Facebook platforms that are dedicated to new mothers: https://www.facebook.com/groups/128315752667473, https://www.facebook.com/groups/1610946472271520/?hoisted_section_header_type=recently_seen&multi_permalinks=7949950545037716
4 This elucidates the unjustness of Manfred Frings' earlier critique, wherein Husserl was faulted for neglecting the developmental trajectory of the ego from birth to maturity (Frings, 1978, p. 146), a perspective challenged by subsequent scholarship.
5 Later republished in "On Female Body Experience: 'Throwing Like a Girl' and Other Essays" (Young, 2005) and contemporaneous research by Louise Levesque-Lopman (Levesque-Lopman, 1983). Noteworthy contributions include those by Depraz (2003) and Heinämaa (2014), alongside collective volumes such as "Coming to Life: Philosophies of Pregnancy, Childbirth, and Mothering" (Adams & Lundquist, 2013) and "Phenomenology of Pregnancy" (Bornemark & Smith, 2016).

6 Reflection on the experience of pregnancy reveals a body subjectivity that is decentered, myself in the mode of not being myself. . . . The first movements of the fetus produce the sense of the splitting subject; the fetus' movements are wholly mine, completely within me, conditioning my experience and space. Only I have access to these movements from their origin, as it were (Young, 1984/1990, pp. 162–163).

7 The pregnant subject . . . experiences her body as herself and not herself. Its inner movements belong to another being, yet they are not other . . . This split subject appears in the eroticism of pregnancy, in which the woman can experience an innocent narcissism fed by recollection of her repressed experience of her own mother's body . . . . The first movements of the fetus produce the sense of the splitting subject; the fetus' movements are wholly mine, completely within me, conditioning my experience and space. Only I have access to these movements from their origin, as it were (Young, 1984/1990, pp. 160–162).

8 "auf die Mutter in der Genesis von Anfang an" Husserl (2014, p. 461).

9 Interestingly, the word obstetric comes from ob-stare, to hinder, stand at, to prevent.

10 Hua-Mat VIII, p. 84: "Temporalization of the concrete present as impressional present of persisting unities and pluralities . . . [it] is the first and more original temporalization of the time-mode present, and then of the time-mode past".

11 https://www.hodinkee.com/articles/how-motherhood-changed-my-perception-of-time

12 For Merleau-Ponty, the projects of my body always seem to serve my own interests: "I want to go over there, and here I am. . . . I look at the goal, I am drawn by it, and the bodily apparatus" follows (1995, p. 9). Hence, exhaustion blocks the functioning of the body, while Sartre obliges the subject to withdraw from one's own bodily interaction and project. Sartre illustrates fatigue through this example: "I start out on a hike with friends. At the end of several hours of walking my fatigue increases. . . . At first I resist and then suddenly I let myself go, I give up, I throw my knapsack down on the side of the road". This gradual release of what one is trying to hold on to, loosening one's grip even as it tightens, characterizes fatigue—it is not just the cause of this release but the release itself (1995, p. 9).

References

Adams, S. L., & Lundquist, C. R. (Eds.). (2013). *Coming to life: Philosophies of pregnancy, childbirth, and mothering.* Fordham University Press.

Alsén, S., Ali, L., Ekman, I., & Fors, A. (2020). Facing a blind alley – Experiences of stress-related exhaustion: A qualitative study. *BMJ Open, 10*(9), e038230.

Beauvoir, S. (1987). *The second sex* (H. M. Parshley, Trans.). Penguin. (Original work published 1949)

Bergum. (1986). *The phenomenology of woman to mother* [Doctoral dissertation, University of Alberta, unpublished]. https://era.library.ualberta.ca/items/5bd71ea9-8026-4712-8865-ed8d6da810c2

Bornemark, J., & Smith, N. (Eds.). (2016). *Phenomenology of pregnancy* (Södertörn Philosophical Studies).

Brentano, F. (1995). *Psychology from an empirical standpoint* (L. L. McAlister, Ed. & A. C. Rancurello et al., Trans.). Routledge.

Butler, J. (1988). Performative acts and gender constitution: An essay in phenomenology and feminist theory. *Theatre Journal, 40*, 519–531.

Chesler, P. (1979). *With child. Diary of motherhood.* Penguin.

Depraz, N. (2003). The intimate other. A phenomenology of lucid embodiment in the light of the lived experience of pregnancy. *Theoria et Historia Scientiarum, 1*, 163–179.

DiPietro, J. A., Voegtline, K. M., Costigan, K. A., Aguirre, F., Kivlighan, K., & Chen, P. (2013). Physiological reactivity of pregnant women to evoked fetal startle. *Journal of Psychosomatic Research, 75*, 321–326.

Frings, M. (1978). Husserl and Scheler: Two views on intersubjectivity. *Journal of the British Society for Phenomenology, 9*(3), 143–149.

Fuchs, T., & Koch, S. C. (2014). *Embodied affectivity: On moving and being moved.* Springer.

Grumet, M. (1983). My face is thine eye, thine in mine appears: The look of parenting and pedagogy. *Phenomenology + Pedagogy, 1*(1), 45–58.

Gurwitsch, A. (1966). *Studies in phenomenology and psychology.* North-western University Press.

Hartmann, N. (1985). *Zur Grundlegung der Ontologie.* De Gruyter.

Hatfield, E., Traore, S. A., & Diarra, S. (1994). *Emotional contagion.* Cambridge University Press.

Heidegger, M. (1996). *Being and time* (J. Stambaugh, Trans.). State University of New York Press.

Husserl, E. (2001). *Logical investigations, first volume: Prolegomena to pure logic, investigations I and II* (J. N. Findlay, Trans.). Routledge.

Heinämaa, S. (2014). 'An equivocal couple overwhelmed by life:' A phenomenological analysis of pregnancy. *Philosophia, 4*, 31–49.

Heinämaa, S. (2020). Values of love: Two forms of infinity characteristic of human persons. *Phenomenology and the Cognitive Sciences.* https://doi.org/10.1007/s11097-019-09653-2

Husserl, E. (1970). *The crisis of European sciences and transcendental phenomenology* (D. Carr, Trans.). Northwestern University Press.

Husserl, E. (1973). *Zur Phänomenologie der Intersubjektivität. Texte aus dem Nachlass. Zweiter Teil: 1921–1928. Husserliana, vol. XIV (Hua XIV)* (I. Kern, Ed.). Martinus Nijhoff.

Husserl, E. (Hua28) (1988). *Vorlesungen über Ethik und Wertlehre 1908–1914, Husserliana XXVIII.* (U. Melle, Ed.) Kluwer Academic Publishers.

Husserl, E. (2014). *Grenzprobleme der Phänomenologie: Analysen des Unbewußtseins und der Instinkte, Metaphysik, späte Ethik: Texte aus dem Nachlass (1908–1937). Husserliana, vol. XLII (Hua XLII)* (R. Sowa & T. Vongehr, Eds.). Springer.

Katz, E. (2004). From Eros to maternity: Love, death, and 'the feminine' in the philosophy of Emmanuel Lévinas. In H. Tirosh-Samuelson (Ed.), *Women and gender in Jewish philosophy* (pp. 153–175). Indiana University Press.

Kristeva, J. (1980). Motherhood according to Bellini. In T. Gora, A. Jardine, & L. S. Roudiez (Eds.), *Desire in language: A semiotic approach to literature and art* (pp. 3–17). Columbia University Press. (Original work published 1977)

Levesque-Lopman, L. (1983). Decision and experience: A phenomenological analysis of pregnancy and childbirth. *Human Studies, 6*, 247–277.

Levinas, E. (1969). *Totality and infinity* (A. Lingis, Trans.). Duquesne University Press.

Lymer, J. (2011). Merleau-Ponty and the affective maternal-foetal relation. *Parrhesia, 13*, 126–143.

Marx, V., & Nagy, E. (2015). Fetal behavioural responses to maternal voice and touch. *PloS one, 10*(6), e0129118.

Merleau-Ponty, M. (1995). *Phenomenology of perception* (C. Smith, Trans.). Routledge & Kegan Paul. (Original work published 1945)

Miglio, N. (2019). Affective schemas, gestational incorporation, and fetal-maternal touch: A Husserlian inquiry. Humana Mente. *Journal of Philosophical Studies, 36*, 67–99.

Moran, D. (2013). Intentionality: Some lessons from the history of the problem from Brentano to the present. *International Journal of Philosophical Studies, 21*(3), 317–358.

Morny, R. (1994). Lévinas: Alterity, the feminine and women—A meditation. *Studies in Religion, 22*, 463–485.

Moustakas, C. (1961). *Loneliness*. Prentice Hall.

Neuhmann, E. (1955). *The great mother*. Princeton University Press.

Oakley, A. (1980). *Becoming a mother*. Time Tested Books.

Odent, M. (1981, Spring). The evolution of obstetrics at Pithivers. *Birth and the Family Journal, 1*(8), 7–15.

Oksala, J. (2003). The birth of man. In D. Zahavi, S. Heinämaa, & H. Ruin (Eds.), *Metaphysics, facticity, interpretation: Phenomenology in the Nordic countries* (pp. 139–166). Kluwer.

Quintero, A. M., & De Jaegher, H. (2020). Pregnant agencies: Movement and participation in maternal-fetal interactions. *Frontiers in Psychology, 11*, 1977.

Ricoeur, P. (1990). *Time and narative*. University of Chicago Press.

Ruddick, S. (1989). *Maternal thinking: Toward a politics of peace*. Beacon Press.

Sartre, J.-P. (1986). *Being and nothingness* (H. E. Barnes, Trans.). Routledge.

Scheler, M. (1954). *Der Formalismus in der Ethik und die materiale Wertethik. Gesammelte Werke, Band II (GW 2)*. Francke Verlag.

Schües, C. (1997). jThe birth of difference. *Human Studies, 20*, 243–252.

Schües, C. (2000). Empirical and transcendental subjectivity: An enigmatic relation? In B. Gupta (Ed.), *The empirical and the transcendental: A fusion of horizons* (pp. 103–117). Rowman & Littlefield.

Serban, C. (2024). *From tendencies and drives to affectivity and ethics: Husserl and Scheler on the mother–child relationship*. Human Studies.

Smith, N. (2016). Phenomenology of pregnancy: A cure for philosophy? In J. Bornemark & N. Smith (Eds.), *Phenomenology of pregnancy* (pp. 15–49). Södertörn Philosophical Studies.

Sowa, R. (2007). Wesen und Wesensgesetze in der deskriptiven Eidetik Husserls. *Phänomenologische Forschungen, 2007*(1), 5–37.

Stein, E. (1970). *On the problem of empathy*. The Hague.

Summa, M., Klein, M., & Schmidt, P. (2022). Introduction: Double Intentionality. *Topoi, 41*, 93–109.

Tordoff, D. M., Moseson, H., Ragosta, S., Hastings, J., Flentje, A., Capriotti, M. R., Lubensky, M. E., Lunn, M. R., & Obedin-Maliver, J. (2023). Family building and pregnancy experiences of cisgender sexual minority women. *AJOG Global Reports, 4*(1), 100298.

Woodman, M. (1985). *The pregnant virgin: A process of psychological transformation*. Inner City Books.

Young, I. M. (1984). Pregnant embodiment: Subjectivity and alienation. *The Journal of Medicine and Philosophy: A Forum for Bioethics and Philosophy of Medicine, 9*(1), 45–62.

Young, I. M. (2005). On female body experience. In *Throwing like a girl and other essays*. Oxford University Press.

Zajonc, R. B. (1980). Feeling and thinking: Preferences need no inferences. *American Psychologist, 35*, 151–175.

6

WOMEN WHO COME BACK

Reconnecting With One's Resources, Space and Time

I. Introduction

Who do we become from the moment the pregnancy test turns positive, and how does this shape our identity thereafter? The change is in front of everyone, but the words to describe the moments that make this revolution possible are so difficult to find that women seem to always remain silent with respect to their individual story (Carpenter & Austin, 2007). Pregnant bodies are typically conspicuous, easily noticed by others. However, the visibility of women in the postpartum period is significantly reduced. This is evident when a woman who has recently given birth walks down the street, and it becomes even more pronounced when one seeks representation of postpartum experiences in pregnancy and childbirth literature. The lack of information about women postpartum and their fourth trimester reflects the pattern of invisibility and silence that they live in their lives. After delivery, the focus shifts from the woman to the survival of the baby—as if this survival no longer concerns her. The postpartum woman walking on the street is still carrying her baby with her, although not visibly. This excerpt from Kana is significant to emphasize the double psychological migration of herself and her mother:

> During my pregnancy, I dreamed a lot about my family in Japan and the place I grew up. I "went back" to the apartment where I lived between 0 to 16-year-old, almost every night in my dreams. When I was 2 months pregnant, I dreamed when I was 3 year old, at 5 months pregnant I was 7 year old in my dream, then at 8 months pregnant, I was 10 years old in my dream, and so on. I felt like I was going through my early life again. It was in chronological

DOI: 10.4324/9781003490937-6

order. My mother was a very generous person, but she had some kind of problem ignoring the facts in front of her: for example, she rarely asked what I did at school every day. She struggled a lot to decide what to prioritize in her life, career, or household/growing children. She cared a lot about her social status. It was important for her that people continue considering her as "an independent working woman" even after having children. Until a very early age like 3, my mother stayed with me at home. However, after I started to go to school, she was often absent at home. Sometimes she came back home around 9 or 10 pm. That is the reason why I wish to stay with my child as much as possible. I missed my mother at home.

In Kana's story, she visited herself as her appointment to motherhood got closer and interrogated herself about her mother's distance. Similarly, this chapter wants to give words to that remoteness and invisibility in order to track the psychological migration of women from themselves to a new self in the important transition to motherhood, mainly to address these two questions: where do we go when we leave? To whom do we come back if we come back? To this purpose, the chapter will discuss what I called the paradox of aloneness to depict the common predicament in which women find no longer time to be alone by themselves, but at the same time they feel a sense of loneliness even when with other people. From there, I briefly discuss the theme of death as a metaphor for the radical transition to motherhood. For this purpose, the folk tale Sealskin, Soulskin, as narrated by Pinkola Estés (1995), will be used to see how time becomes the place where the body of the woman disappears and finds its way back. Both the notion of time and the notion of body will be analyzed using a Husserlian perspective.

II. The Paradox of Aloneness

The hermeneutic efforts to shape the narrative of birth often result in a loss for words to precisely describe women's transformative experiences (Lundgren & Wahlberg, 1999). When everything goes well—that is, when the baby was planned and the parents can hold a healthy baby after nine months of healthy gestation—smiles, photos, short texts and confusing visits from relatives and friends become the ways in which the birth story starts to unfold. Gradually, and often in a disorganized manner, a narrative takes shape, punctuated by a few repeated questions: when did labor start? How many hours did it last? Was the baby born via C-section or natural delivery? Are you both healthy? (Although this last question often focuses more on the health of the newborn.) (Oakley, 1984).

The story seems to begin and end around these few narrative clues. However, anyone who has welcomed a baby into their home knows that this is not the entire story, and what is truly occurring in their lives is almost impossible to convey. As Marinopoulos beautifully wrote (2005, p. 12):

> Mothers suffer in silence and they do not talk about it. That is no news. Each moment in history built its own silence closing a part of humanity in a universe with no words. Women are those who remained silent the longest about this intimate lived experience that concerns themselves in a moment that is as commonly shared and at the same time as lonely as the birth of a child.

What makes it difficult to create one's own convincing narrative, rather than relying on stories passed down from previous generations (Kay et al., 2017), is what I would define as the paradox of aloneness. This paradox arises from the sudden lack of alone time that a new parent experiences. This absence of solitude hinders one's ability to wrap their mind around recent events and to reassemble their psychological pieces in order to feel whole again. In essence, there is no unified self capable of finding the right words to tell the story. There is no time to be alone and to collect the pieces of oneself left fragmented after such a powerful event.

An important connection with one's intimate space, from which words should emerge, is continuously postponed by the pressing daily chores required to care for the new life. This obstruction of sense creates a space of loneliness (Taylor et al., 2021; Mandai et al., 2018), where a deep silence grows. It becomes pointless or exhausting (Prizeman et al., 2023) to try to find words to express how one really feels, resulting in a strange sense of uneasiness within one's own skin. Despite always being together with a new life, the sense of loneliness, anxiety and stress becomes pervasive, as in Maren's story:

> 6 weeks after birth, I went with little Emma for the first time for a walk in the stroller to my last appointment with the midwife. I was so tensed, alert, and anxious that she would begin to cry again (what they do when they are not used to being ride around with a stroller) that lost my way, came late, covered in sweat, and felt exhausted. In retrospect I cannot imagine why this was so difficult or why I was so anxious or tensed, as you get used to the crying and are able to anticipate the behavior of your little one, you know when it is serious and when it is just a crying hour. This continuous tension and alertness were unbearable, I felt as if I was going to get crazy or psychotic. It went worse when Emma was seriously sick for the first time. One night, when she was coughing a lot and stopped breathing for a moment, Michel and me immediately had the feeling, ok, this is serious. But I was so anxious and in panic that I couldn't react properly, my whole body was shaking, luckily, he did the right thing, calling the weekend ambulance, organizing a drive (we do not have a car) and getting her to the doctor. In the end, everything turned

out fine, but I couldn't sleep for the next two weeks, every time she coughed or showed any sign of sickness, I started shivering and panicking again. This only ended, after she turned 5 months, and I stopped breast feeding, and the hormones went back to normal.

Within this sentiment of confusion and transformation, an important theme emerges: death, conceived as an ideation or metaphorical deep transition (LaSusa, 2021; Adlington et al., 2023).

II.1 The Theme of Death and One Origin of Femicide

The concept of psychological death in pregnant mothers (Chin et al., 2022) speaks to the profound emotional and psychological upheaval that some women experience during pregnancy. This term does not indicate a literal death but rather a metaphorical one, capturing the profound changes and transformations that reshape a woman's life and identity as she steps into motherhood (Laney et al., 2015). This experience often involves a sense of losing one's pre-pregnancy identity, accompanied by feelings of mourning for the life and freedoms that once were (Lau et al., 2022). This process is marked by a deep sense of responsibility and the sobering realization that life will be forever altered once the baby arrives (Thompson et al., 2018).

This psychological death arises from the confluence of factors. The first is the profound transformation of identity, a theme we explored in earlier chapters. Pregnancy initiates a significant shift, not just physically but psychologically, as a woman readies herself to become a mother. This metamorphosis can lead to feelings of confusion and loss as she navigates her evolving sense of self.

Then there is the fear of the unknown, a concept we delved into in Chapter 3. Pregnancy, particularly for first-time mothers, can be a journey filled with uncertainties. The weight of the unknown and the immense responsibility of nurturing a new life can evoke feelings of psychological death as women confront the challenges and changes that lie ahead (Hassanzadeh et al., 2020).

Physical and emotional changes further complicate this experience. As highlighted in the narratives we explored in the first chapter, pregnancy brings hormonal shifts and physical transformations that significantly impact a woman's emotional well-being. These hormonal fluctuations can lead to mood swings and heightened emotions, adding layers of complexity to the psychological experience (Gokce Isbir, 2016). Trifu et al. (2019) notes that the hormonal changes during pregnancy can mimic conditions like hyperthyroidism, pituitary adenoma, Cushing's disease and diabetes mellitus, all of which are associated with psychiatric disturbances.

The sense of loss, or matrescence, also plays a pivotal role. The journey to motherhood often demands the sacrifice of certain aspects of one's previous life—personal time, hobbies or career pursuits. This can lead to grieving for what has been lost and finding it emotionally challenging to embrace new paths in practical and emotional life (Sacks, 2017; Stern et al., 1998).

Ambivalence is another layer to this complex experience. While pregnancy can bring joy and anticipation, it is also normal for pregnant mothers to experience conflicting emotions. They may feel ambivalent about becoming a mother or worry about their ability to fulfill their maternal role (Athan & Reel, 2015; Wekesa et al., 2018).

Lastly, Mother Imposter Syndrome can shadow this journey. Women approaching this new aspect of their identity may feel like frauds, fearing that others will uncover their perceived limitations and failures (Mir, 2022). Embracing these feelings and being able to go with the rapid flow of these changes is part of motherhood. As Elliott wrote, parenthood is not for the lazy and weak:

> Parenting is a dynamic process. It is fluid and never static. Every moment is unique and changes you. I have come to realize that much like the times I would put an outfit on my child and see that it was too small and wonder how they grew so fast because it fit just last week, I am also growing and changing as quickly.
>
> Parenting is not for the weak and lazy. Parenting is a master class for those that are willing to learn. The first realization is that parenting is about reparenting yourself. There is a fundamental shift in the scripts and stories that one grows up with and how they understand themselves. Once you become a parent, it is impossible not to reflect on the experiences you had with your parents—for better or worse—and try to make judgements about whether or not you will align with those experiences. You begin to rethink and reformulate your own childhood. You reposition yourself in your own memory as you make choices about how to move ahead with your child and must reconsider the conditions your own parents were in as they made choices that might have confused you. It is this remembering and recontextualizing that forces you to change your positionality on your whole being and history.

The elements that intertwine in the transformation toward motherhood contribute to the rebirth of identity; the old self, with its personal name, must make space for a new, egoless self born alongside the new baby. The individual identity coexists with a universal role—the name "mum" uttered by the child, a word that, while universal, uniquely designates the mother. This clash between universality and particularity seeks harmony in the process.

In fact, if the process of rebirth does not properly unfold, the risk is to be sucked up into the universality of the name, mother, and consequently fall into a performative character where engendering (MacMahon, 1995) and performative (Butler, 1988) tasks prevail over the true needs and desires of the mother. It might in fact happen that instead of expressing their true selves, women would behave as is expected from them according to their social background. According to McMahon, women often find themselves being engendered by motherhood in culturally variable ways. Middle-class women felt that motherhood had changed their personal sense of themselves, that they had become morally transformed into less selfish, more caring people by virtue of their emotional connection to their children. The working-class women approached this self-transformation in terms of "responsibilities" and "settling down". McMahon describes it as "moral reform"; for many of the working-class women, motherhood was perceived as signaling the death of the old self—funny or crazy or free—and its replacement with (or redemption by) the mothers (MacMahon, 1995).

Unfortunately, when this role is embraced through an infinite series of demanded sacrifices, death does not arise as a spontaneous process of renewal but as a dangerous signal of femicide and violence against women. When this occurs, the transition to motherhood becomes a derogatory way of treating women by just demanding a certain array of services and behaviors. In this case, the family becomes a dysfunctional place where children learn how to belittle and overlook the role that the woman expects in society. As Roberts' data[1] shows (2023), often femicide starts at home, when the abnegation of the woman toward her family and her offspring is sanctified and expected as the only regulative model for a functioning family. This is to say that even though the woman has necessarily to go through a radical transformation, when this transformation is demanded without honoring the time and space needed by the woman to mourn the pieces of self that she has to let go, this metaphorical death comes in a very violent way. This way of transformation shows, in fact, to the family and especially to their prole a dangerous model of abnegation both for boys and for girls. In fact, girls would learn that this level of sacrifice is the one expected when loving deeply someone; conversely, boys would think that it is right to demand that much from women when being loved.

For this reason, in the next section, I will reflect on how we can allow a smoother transition through this radical transformation. In order to address the questions raised in the introduction and keep track of the soul migratory process of women during this transformative transition to motherhood, I will use Pinkola's analysis of the tale Sealskin, Soulskin.

III. The Story of "Sealskin, Soulskin"

In "Women Who Run with the Wolves", a book written by Pinkola Estés, there is a retelling of the traditional folk tale titled "Sealskin, Soulskin". The story revolves around a young woman who possesses a magical sealskin that allows her to transform into a seal and live in the sea.

The tale begins with a very lonely fisherman discovering the sealskin on the beach and taking it home with him. When he arrives at his house, the sealskin transforms into a beautiful young woman. The fisherman is captivated by her enchanting beauty and decides to marry her. They live together and have children, but the woman always longs for the sea and her seal form.

One day, the fisherman goes out to sea, leaving his wife and children behind. The woman's yearning for the sea becomes unbearable, and she can no longer resist the call of the ocean. In her husband's absence, she finds the hidden sealskin and, driven by her longing, puts it on. Instantly, she transforms back into a seal and returns to her true home in the sea.

The fisherman returns home to find his wife missing and the sealskin gone. He is devastated by the loss of his beloved wife and searches everywhere for her. Despite his efforts, he cannot find her or the sealskin.

Years pass, and the woman continues to live happily as a seal in the sea. However, she never forgets her husband and children on land. One day, she hears a song carried by the waves, telling the story of a fisherman who lost his wife to the sea. The woman recognizes the song and realizes that it is about her own past.

Torn between her love for her family and her longing for the sea, the woman makes a difficult decision. She returns to the shore and transforms back into her human form, donning her "soulskin", which symbolizes her human identity and connection to her family.

The woman goes to find her husband, who is overjoyed to see her again. She explains that she not only loves him and their children but also needs to be true to her own nature as a seal. Recognizing the depth of her love and the truth of her dual identity, the fisherman accepts her decision.

From that day on, the woman spends part of her time with her family on land and part of her time in the sea as a seal. She learns to balance her two identities, living as both a human and a creature of the sea, and finds fulfillment in embracing her true self.

III.1 Coming Back

The tale of "Sealskin, Soulskin" explores several themes, such as those of longing, identity and the importance of honoring one's true nature. From this story, we learn how necessary it is to accept and integrate all aspects of oneself, even if they seem contradictory, in order to find wholeness and happiness. This kind of *hap*piness happens when we become capable of being ourselves; that is, when we honor the boundaries that separate our inner worlds. It is "an happening" because we need to be open to letting go of the volitions of our ego (see Chapter 4) and letting life do its job in shaping the flow of our being. We do not have control over it except by honoring what is happening to us and letting it be. In fact, in Pinkola Estés' analysis, what stands out is the image of the lonely husband, which represents our ego alluring us to get further and further away from us to reach in exchange for a togetherness we crave and a sense of completeness and perfection (this echoes with Maren's story, who decided to have children with her partner because he would not have needed a child to feel complete. The allurement of the ego, in that sense, was partly neutralized in her case). In that togetherness, though, we find ourselves even lonelier than before—what we called before the paradox of aloneness. As she writes:

> Eventually every woman who stays away from her soul-home for too long, tires. This is as it should be. Then she seeks her skin again in order to revive her sense of self and soul, in order to restore her deep-eyed and oceanic knowing.
>
> *(1995, p. 159)*

To refer to the paradox I aforementioned, we need to come back to a state of aloneness in order to overcome loneliness and revive an intimate sense of self from which we can restore wholeness and togetherness with the world. As she continues,

> We fervently point out how other creatures' natural territories have become surrounded by cities, ranches, highways, noise, and other dissonance, as though we are not surrounded by the same, as though we are not affected also. We know that for creatures to live on, they must at least from time to time have a home place, a place where they feel both protected and free.
>
> *(1996, p. 160)*

While we know of this for natural creatures, we forget about this when it comes to our nature and our deepest needs. We forget our need to come back to a home place where we can feel protected, free and respected for who we are. There is almost a sense of shame, or even a sense of monstrosity, around the need to reconnect with one's own nature.

In the tale, the martial bond sealed with the birth of their beloved children allures her into forgetting about her dual nature, which, even with contrasts and contradictions, needs to be honored and respected in order to remain alive. Instead of killing her feminine nature, the children, the youngest and most natural part of her, maybe a representation of her instincts, honor her nature and will eventually learn from her example how to live across the two worlds; they will come out enriched from this acceptance.

From this, it emerges with a certain emphasis the theme of coming back, as Pinkola Estés remarks: "This great cycle of going and returning, going and returning, is reflexive within the instinctual nature" (1995, p. 159). We need to go out of our comfort zone to please our ego and accomplish our identity as much as we need to come back to our instinctive soul in order to be in our skin and nurture who we really are, despite the bonds and important relationships we create in life.

In the case of this tale, the ego is a thief whose damage we can limitate if we learn how to go with this cycle. The husband sees this beautiful sealskin on the beach and wants it for himself. As in Pinkola Estes' interpretation, "This big theft can, with consciousness, be mediated in the future if we will pay attention to our cycles and the call to take leave and return home (1995, p. 160). There would be no theft or unaware loss if we learned to pay attention to the contrasting and yet legitimate needs to feel at home, free and safe.

Reflecting on the questions raised in the introduction, what kind of theft do we encounter when giving birth to a child? To whom do we come back? And, who are we when we come back? As Pinkola Estés writes, "The aggravated theft of the sealskin also occurs far more subtly through the theft of a woman's resources and of her time" (1995, p. 160). As I will explain more in depth in the next sections using Husserl's phenomenological perspective, when we let our time be swallowed in the event of birth, our agentic body, too, that animates and populates our own world, disappears in this living present. This kind of metaphorical death would leave no space for a coming back and a deep transformation to happen. To keep the cycle open, we need to learn how to recover that time and, with it, our agency.

IV. Time for Leaving

Where do we go when we leave? In the tale of the sealskin soulskin, the protagonist loses track of time, leading her to forget her skills and personal resources. Leaving her marine life, she first abandons a space where she could enjoy her own time, entering instead an ever-present instant filled with the magic of the new life she created for herself and her children. Time, by its very nature, can profoundly shape one's life. It is not merely a quality of being; it is being itself, as emphasized in Husserl's phenomenological perspective, among others.

In the Bernau and C manuscripts on time, Husserl uses the terms "phenomenological time" and "phenomenic time" to distinguish different aspects of time-consciousness. Phenomenological time refers to the structure of time-consciousness as a lived experience, analyzed reflectively to uncover the essential features of temporal consciousness, including how past experiences are retained, how the present unfolds and how future anticipations arise. In this sense, phenomenological time examines the lived experience of time as it manifests in our consciousness. On the other hand, phenomenic time refers to time as an objective, external concept that can be studied scientifically or mathematically. It is the time that appears in the physical world, measurable and quantifiable, such as clock time or the time measured by physical events like the movement of celestial bodies. Phenomenic time is studied and understood in the context of natural sciences, distinct from the first-person experience of time that Husserl investigates in his phenomenology. The phenomenological sense of time is explained through the structure of a now that looks toward the future through protentions and retains some of the past through retentions. Retentions and protentions explain how past and future moments persist and are anticipated in the lived experience of our consciousness. In his "Ideas", he elucidates that "[r]etention and protention are essential features of our experience, allowing for the temporal unity of consciousness" (Husserl, 1931, p. 38). These temporal elements create a seamless "stream of consciousness connecting past, present, and future in a continuous flow" (Husserl, 1966, p. 51).

Giving birth becomes a practical form of phenomenological practice, called epoché and reduction. By giving birth, women have to put in parentheses all the assumptions and preconceived beliefs that structured their previous life (epoché) and find the essence defining their being in that new phase of life (reduction). In doing so, they dwell in a phenomenological sense of time, the ever-present now that annuls any sense of phenomenic objective time. As we read in the stories collected in the first chapter, the time indicated on the watch or by the passing of the day becomes a mere background to what is truly happening—the pure manifestation of life itself. For instance, the days of labor or the sleepless nights disclose a primordial level of streaming living present in which women live without any reference to objective time. Moreover, on this level, the woman discovers herself as a being in relation to another being. The "I" does not relate only to itself in an unaware identity but is a reflective I capable of seeing itself and the "Other"; that is, at this deepest level of time consciousness, the subject is intrinsically intersubjective. At its deepest level of manifestation, life is time, meant as an intersubjective flow of being.

Husserl describes this level as one of "coincidence with Others on an original level of constitution, my coincidence, so to speak, before there is constituted a world for myself and other"; at this level, the ego is "not mine in opposition to that of other humans, and it is not mine as that of a body-soul existent, that of a real human" (Manuscript C 3, 3b). When we are living an experience at its most original level, whether it be the experience of falling in love or going through a life-threatening event, the experience does not belong to me or you in a separate fashion. As Maren recounts:

> The whole thing is not about you, your pain, body or state of mind is not as important, your body is in the service of giving birth, the main medical goal is to guarantee the survival and successful birth of the child (which includes your well-being to a certain extent of course). Things are being done with you and decisions over your body are being made, at times without being communicated or explained to you.

What is happening does not properly belong to me but serves something that transcends me. My time of experiencing something will be distinguished from that lived by my baby or my family only later, when I thematize my experience and find a meaning that might differ from others'. At its primordial level, comparable to the time of labor, the time of experience is anonymous and radically pre-egoic (Husserl, 1973, p. 598). Husserl explains it with these words:

> [I]n the stream of the living present [the ego-pole] is the identical persisting pole in the changes of the immanent temporal occurrences . . . this pure "I" is abstract, it is only concrete through the content of the streaming present.
>
> *(C 3, 42a)*

What exists in the ever-present moments of a newborn's first hours or during a woman's labor is an ego that can be compared to an abstraction or, more metaphorically, to a chameleon, whose content and shape continually change according to the immediate experience. In this sense, it becomes concrete only through the content manifested in the streaming present—"I am my push; I am this life that has just come into being; I am the ceiling I am staring at while the doctor performs my c-section".

This form of "I" cannot be named as you or me. "The primal-ego carries in itself the counterpart, the existing, having-become ego and its surroundings, what is there for this and for me as an anonymous ego, as non-ego" (C 2, 3a/b). This ego stands as what is for it—in this case, the life of the newborn.

At this deep level, the functioning of the woman's body is driven by two main instincts: objectification (C 13 I, 136) and intersubjectivity. In the former, the subject is called to receive all the data that comes to experience and store them as a form of passive knowledge. At this stage, the subject is an object among other objects, finding its way to survival by adjusting to the continually new information it receives. Regarding the second level of instincts, Husserl maintains that there is "an instinctive primal intentionality of communalization which pre-grounds the constitution of community and in which there is a pre-awareness of community among different particulars, nevertheless ones which are bound in different particularities and still connectednesses" (E III 10, Sb).

As described in Chapter 4, from the living present of the "I" stem habits that contribute to the unity of the new character of the person. The repeated attitudes the ego takes toward the world are progressively sedimented to form the personality that clothes the ego. This is how an ego actively maintains its own identity in the ever-changing situations of its existence. These attitudes can range from a simple reaction to something to a complex decision-making process that the ego has repeatedly performed. We become who we are because of the habitualities arising in these ever-changing situations. In this world, we find ourselves as primal others, and through a pairing process that shows the similarities between ourselves and others, we realize that there are others with whom we can associate.

The problem we encounter during childbirth is that these two instinctive drives point to a world of rebirth and new beginnings where sedimentations are primarily shaped by the event itself, which is still in the present. The new life is an ever-present moment that renews itself with each step of its growth. It is an event that happens in time and generates a new intimate connection. The mother is absorbed in the care needed for her child's survival, so the habits formed to maintain her character actually point to the character of herself and her baby. This does not tap into her personal skills and resources but into what she is as a primordial being, as an intersubjective living presence. Similarly, in the Seal-skin, Soulskin tale, the protagonist disappears in time, where her resources and skills are forgotten. Her body becomes an object among other objects, seeking survival for herself and her baby, and the community she encounters is primarily populated by herself and her baby.

IV.1 The Event of Giving Birth

Husserl's phenomenology of temporality, as developed in his 1905 lectures, provides a profound framework for understanding the subject's intimate connection to events, particularly the event of giving birth. In these lectures, Husserl aims to elucidate what he calls "what is ultimately and truly absolute" (Husserl, 1931, p. 216): the enigmatic intimacy of consciousness and time at the origin of the double constitution of world and subject. The event disrupts the intimate connection between retentions and protentions, breaking the flow of time and drastically altering a person's style of existence (Husserl, 1970, p. 31). In some ways, the event does not merely occur within a world but rather opens up a new world, bringing us into contact with the origin of time and initiating a new flow.

From a certain perspective, and for some women, giving birth is a traumatizing event from whose aftermath they need time to recover (Beck et al., 2018). Philosophically speaking, "being traumatized means continuing to organize your life as if the trauma were still going on—unchanged and immutable, as every new encounter or event is contaminated by the past" (Van der Kolk, 2015, p. 53).

Whether or not giving birth is traumatic, it represents an event that cuts through time as an ever-present moment, repeating itself in both the past and the present. It is in the nature of the event to seize time and drastically alter its course. This makes planning or foreseeing the future difficult because the event severs connections with any protention toward what life might become. The event does not simply happen in the world; it becomes the world, with the world narrowing and expanding within that form of the living present. The structure of the world and the body, as experienced during the event, remains as if the event is ever-present; thus, the subject continues to engage with the world in the same way as their body originally did during the event. In this sense, the two drives previously mentioned—objectification and communalization—tend to keep the woman anchored in that moment. She becomes the event. I am the birth. I am the mother.

Using Fanon's words (1952, p. 185), the body responds according to the body schema that was active in that moment, rooted in the intersubjective instincts Husserl referred to. As discussed in Chapter 5, the bodily schema (Holmes & Spence, 2004; Merleau-Ponty, 1945) refers to the three-dimensional pattern of habituations and automatic responses that the body generates in response to the world, allowing it to engage passively and actively (de Vignemont et al., 2021). In the aftermath of delivery, the body schema may remain shaped by the event of birth, where the future seems unforeseeable and the past has been irrevocably altered. An ongoing reorganization of identity occurs at every moment.

Consequently, this original intersubjective layer of time encompasses a bodily schema where the woman's time and the baby's time generate a unified life-world in which both bodies live in a symbiotic whole. This symbiosis can make it difficult for the woman to regain agency over her own skills—metaphorically speaking, to feel at ease in her own skin. In the next section, I will explain how this interplay of schemas impacts the woman's body and how she can reclaim her own schema, thereby regaining her sense of time and constitutive functions.

IV.2   Visceral and Opaque Body: Time to Come Back

The opaque body refers to an essential feature of our perceptual experience, wherein certain aspects of an object or body are not immediately accessible to consciousness. When we perceive an object, such as a physical body (Koerper), we encounter its appearance or surface features directly. However, Husserl points out that our perception is limited in that we do not have immediate access to the inner or hidden aspects of the object. For example, when we see someone's body, we perceive its visible features like color, shape and texture, but we do not directly perceive their internal organs or sensations. The visible aspects of the body belong to the object as we intend it in our perception. However, the body's inner experiences, sensations and private consciousness belong to how the person experiences it and becomes aware of it.

The opaque body serves to highlight how our perceptual experiences, since always directed toward appearances of phenomena, do not grant us immediate access to the inner experiences of the object itself. When giving birth, our own body becomes even more opaque to us. Its infinite variations are unpredictable to us as the body experiences the event of giving birth to a new life in a way that we can barely interpret. Through this event and in the following time, the woman's body exists in a living present where the main instincts, as we saw earlier, are toward objectification and intersubjectivity. On the one hand, her body perceives itself and others as similar objects, and on the other, it tends to experience itself as an "I-we", as a subject together with and similar to a related other.

While in close connection and almost symbiotic unity with the infant's body to ensure its survival, the mother's body learns what it is telling her about her biological changes. This is why many studies refer to the changes occurring in the mother's brain (Oatridge et al., 2002) as a temporary alteration from its normal state. Instead of calling this state "pregnancy brain" (Hoekzema et al., 2017) or referring to it as a state of obfuscation or fog (Barha & Galea, 2017), I would say that at this moment, the body and its neurological system are learning many new things necessary for survival. In this primordial mode of presence, the body perceives itself as instrumental for the survival of a related other.

Leder (1990) coined the term "visceral body" to describe the body's functioning according to its needs and limits; the visceral body makes the basic functioning of life possible, such as breathing, heartbeat and the operation of the stomach and bowels. The visceral body is the primordial presence in time of our opaque body, demanding from us what we viscerally need to survive (eating, sleeping, taking care of our basic well-being).

During pregnancy and after delivery, when women seem to withdraw into an inaccessible space, they might be inhabiting this primordial living present where their visceral body poses very specific and ongoing demands on them. Yet, this visceral body might be opaque to them—it is an object whose experiences are difficult to decipher by themselves. After delivering a baby, the needs of the visceral body are so primal and pressing that they take up the space of subjectivity; these needs demand to become the subject in order to be fulfilled for survival. Osler (2021) notes that when a subject is hungry, this visceral body as an object not only calls attention to itself as an object but also makes demands upon the body as a subject. This means there is an ongoing interplay between the body as object and the body as subject to fulfill life's needs in a functional way. If I experience pain, the body as an object calls the attention of the body as subject to resolve the pain. Even though opaque, the visceral body gives the body as subject clues to engage in the world in a functional way. That is why a diminished sense of ownership of the body might lead to severe dysfunctions in the way we can operate according to our talents. When subjected to extreme fatigue and labor—which often happens when generating life and caring for its survival—we are caught in this double bodily life, mirrored in the two deepest drives found in the primordial presence of time: the biological presence to understand how to survive in the world we are surrounded by as, so to speak, the object of life; and the political presence, which involves our intersubjective instinct to associate with others (where the primal other can just be ourselves) and find in the polis (or inner citadel) our well-being. These two instincts leave little space for the woman's old personality or the exploration of her talents and resources. They are strongly focused on the ever-present event—I became a mother.

As MacMahon (1995) remarks, motherhood is a very personal experience, but it very easily becomes a political matter. The mother herself lives between the visceral instincts dictated by her body and the intersubjective instinct to connect to the other (be it just herself, the child, the family or a supportive group) and hopefully find in it her own forgotten or stolen skin. When this latter step proves unsuccessful, performative acts (Butler, 1988) and engendering (MacMahon, 1995) drift into foreign performative schemas (Fanon, 1952), as the mother, like in the tale, finds her skin in a dimension that does not fully belong to her.

In this sense, it is extremely important to recover ownership of one's own body because this diminished sense of ownership might lead a subject to experience their body as "renegade" and as something that they are "with" rather than something that they "are" (Leder, 2021). By reconnecting with her own talents and resources, the woman dilates the demands of the visceral body and makes her body less opaque. As Hornbacher (2009) writes:

> You stop seeing your body as your own, as something valuable, something that totes you around and does your thinking and feeling for you and requires an input of energy for this favor. You begin seeing it instead as an undesirable appendage, a wart you need to remove.
>
> *(p. 57)*

To avoid this dismissive attitude toward a body that became objectified, physical exercise and self-observation of who we became can be initial steps toward a recovery of personal resources and accordingly agency. In order to recover a bodily schema that is functional to one's own talent, women need to see their body as their own and not as an appendage that obstructs their will. From there, they can recover their movement in time as subjects capable of planning in the future and detaching from a traumatizing past. Hence, accepting the role of the visceral body and trying to decipher its opacity and to understand what it can teach us about our survival can be a tool for the woman to re-own the will and come back to her own skin. That will help to see what that body became and what that body can do for her and no longer for the event of motherhood.

V. To Whom Do We Come Back? Who Are We When We Come Back?

Marinopoulos describes actual maternity as prepared by psychic maternity (2005, p. 19). This means that in order to actually become a mother, we need that the pieces of ourselves come back together to form the wholeness in which we can find a home for ourselves. The event of giving birth breaks that wholeness and the identity of the mother are sucked up in a form of living present where the agentic subject identifies with, or even gets lost in, the visceral body; this latter in fact disrupts the agency of the subject and its ability to live in the world according to its talents and skills. In this modality, the body is the event and is learning how to survive it.

In this dynamic, the instinct for intersubjective community becomes key to recovering a path to that psychic unity. As Marinopoulos remarks, a social body is required for the body of the mother to come back to its entirety and recover the care that is needed to come back (2005, p. 80). The community of women, in the tale of the oceanic underwater community, is key to seeing again our own body and perceiving it as something we are and not as our appendage. The community can be as small as oneself being able to see and accept one's own alterity.

The whole we come back to when and if we find our way back is the wholeness of our own time. By that, I mean the phenomenological time of our experience according to our own sedimented habits; that is, the time in which we find ourselves as persons separated from but intersubjectively connected with the time of our baby. When we come back, we are our own skin, in our own opaque body, whose visceral needs are not necessarily disruptive of our subjective agency but are capable of functioning for our survival and the survival of our babies without pressing demands.

For this to happen, we need, metaphorically speaking, the ocean; as in the tale, we need a strong but flexible social and political structure capable of welcoming our coming back where the event of having a baby and raising them can be supported. As Pinkola Estés wrote:

> Finding the way back to one's rightful psychic order begins with the feeding of or the caring for a lonely and/or injured woman, man, or beast. That such a child, who will have the ability to traverse two very different worlds, can come from a woman who is in such a skinless state and "married" to something in herself or in the outer world that is so lonely and undeveloped is one of the constant miracles of the psyche. Something occurs within us when we are in such a state, something that produces a feeling state, a tiny new life, a small flame that thrives under imperfect, arduous, or even inhumane condition.
>
> *(1995, p. 160)*

To address the questions raised at the beginning of this chapter concerning where we go and to what we return, we can say that we come back to our own time as beings who stretch toward the future and retain the past; we return to an identity in which we can feel whole again. Yet, for this to happen, we need to care about our own alterity and the different worlds we live in. As I stated elsewhere, if society, too, took care of the conditions in which our future generations are raised, we would have fewer psychiatric, social and political emergencies to face in our communities. The woman who comes back needs to find the space to reconnect with her skin, to renounce the status of sainthood, and to find a way to be her new caring self again with others who are not her duties but are beings intersubjectively connected to her by the event that brought them into this world.

VI. Conclusion

In this chapter, I discussed the psychological intricacies of giving birth and finding one's way back to oneself afterward. Using the tale of Sealskin, Soulskin as a metaphorical tool, I provided a narrative for this complex transformation and highlighted how themes of death and even femicide become key elements in this deep process. For the transformative steps following this metaphorical death to occur, a woman needs to reconnect with her skills and resources within her own space and time. Therefore, I explored the notion of time from a Husserlian perspective, demonstrating that the constitutive notion of time for a woman after delivery is that of a living present.

Time becomes an event that persists in the female body as a living present, compelling her to continually reorganize her being according to two main drives: the instinct toward objectification and the instinct toward intersubjectivity. The instinct toward objectification leads her to see her body as opaque and to obey its visceral needs for the survival of both herself and her baby. Meanwhile, the instinct toward intersubjectivity pushes her to see herself and others as an "I-we", striving to live within the community.

When a woman's body lives according to these two instincts, increasingly engaging in a world where visceral needs take precedence over the agentic skills of the living body, she may lose herself and merely perform according to expected duties. The woman who truly comes back is the one whose intersubjective instinct manages to reconnect her with her own "skin", represented in the tale by the reclaiming of her own skills and resources. These skills and resources may have been neglected due to the overwhelming visceral needs associated with giving birth and ensuring the survival of her baby.

Note

1 In the census' ten-year report (2009–2018), 109 (8%) of the total of 1,435 women killed by men were mothers killed by sons, while 11 grandmothers were killed by grandsons over the decade. In the latest Femicide Census statistics shared exclusively with the *Observer*, which is campaigning to end femicide, in 2020, the figure for matricide is 15%—14 killings of mothers and five of grandmothers in a single year, with 28 cases in which the relationship is not yet known. In 2019, 18-year-old Rowan Thompson stabbed his mother, Joanna Thompson, 118 times. He later died in a mental health facility. Sophie Rugge-Price, his aunt, said her sister talked about "walking on eggshells" around her son.

References

Adlington, K., Vasquez, C., Pearce, E., Wilson, C. A., Nowland, R., Taylor, B. L., Spring, S., & Johnson, S. (2023). 'Just snap out of it'—The experience of loneliness in women with perinatal depression: A meta-synthesis of qualitative studies. *BMC Psychiatry*, *23*(1), 110.

Athan, A. M., & Reel, H. L. (2015). Maternal psychology: Reflections on the 20th anniversary of deconstructing developmental psychology. *Feminism & Psychology, 25*(3), 311–325.

Barha, C. K., & Galea, L. A. M. (2017). The maternal 'baby brain' revisited. *Nature Neuroscience, 20*(2), 134–135.

Beck, C. T., Watson, S., & Gable, R. K. (2018). Traumatic childbirth and its aftermath: Is there anything positive? *The Journal of Perinatal Education, 27*(3), 175–184.

Butler, J. (1988). Performative acts and gender constitution: An essay in phenomenology and feminist theory. *Theatre Journal, 40*, 519–531.

Carpenter, L., & Austin, H. (2007). Silenced, silence, silent: Motherhood in the margins. *Qualitative Inquiry, 13*(5), 660–674.

Chin, K., Wendt, A., Bennett, I. M., & Bhat, A. (2022). Suicide and maternal mortality. *Current Psychiatry Reports, 24*(4), 239–275.

de Vignemont, F., Pitron, V., & Alsmith, A. J. T. (2021). What is the body schema? In Y. Ataria, S. Tanaka, & S. Gallagher (Eds.), *Body schema and body image: New directions*. Oxford University Press.

Dol, J., Hughes, B., Bonet, M., Dorey, R., Dorling, J., Grant, A., Langlois, E. V., Monaghan, J., Ollivier, R., Parker, R., Roos, N., Scott, H., Shin, H. D., & Curran, J. (2022). Timing of maternal mortality and severe morbidity during the postpartum period: A systematic review. *JBI Evidence Synthesis, 20*(9), 2119–2194.

Fanon, F. (1952). *Black skin, White masks (Peau noire, masques blancs)* (C. L. Markmann, Trans.). Grove Press.

Gokce Isbir, G., Inci, F., Onal, H., & Yildiz, P. D. (2016). The effects of antenatal education on fear of childbirth, maternal self-efficacy and post-traumatic stress disorder (PTSD) symptoms following childbirth: An experimental study. *Applied Nursing Research, 32*, 227–232.

Hassanzadeh, R., Abbas-Alizadeh, F., Meedya, S., Mohammad-Alizadeh-Charandabi, S., & Mirghafourvand, M. (2020). Fear of childbirth, anxiety and depression in three groups of primiparous pregnant women not attending, irregularly attending and regularly attending childbirth preparation classes. *BMC Women's Health, 20*(1), 180.

Hoekzema, E., Barba-Müller, E., Pozzobon, C., Picado, M., Lucco, F., García-García, D., Soliva, J. C., Tobeña, A., Desco, M., Crone, E. A., Ballesteros, A., Carmona, S., & Vilarroya, O. (2017). Pregnancy leads to long-lasting changes in human brain structure. *Nature Neuroscience, 20*(2), 287–296.

Holmes, N. P., & Spence, C. (2004). The body schema and the multisensory representation(s) of peripersonal space. *Cognitive Processing, 5*(2), 94–105. https://doi.org/10.1007/s10339-004-0013-3

Hornbacher, M. (2009). *Wasted: A memoir of anorexia and bulimia* (Ebook). Harper Collins.

Husserl, E. (1931). *Ideas: General introduction to pure phenomenology* (W. R. B. Gibson, Trans.). Macmillan.

Husserl, E. (1966). *Zur Phänomenologie des inneren Zeitbewußtseins* (R. Boehm, Ed.). Martinus Nijhoff.

Husserl, E. (1970). *Crisis of European sciences and transcendental phenomenology* (D. Carr, Ed.). Northwestern Press. (Husserliana VI)

Husserl, E. (1973). *Zur Phanomenologie der Intersubjectiuitat, Dritter Teil: 1929–1935.* Martinus Nijhoff.

Kay, L., Downe, S., Thomson, G., & Finlayson, K. (2017). Engaging with birth stories in pregnancy: A hermeneutic phenomenological study of women's experiences across two generations. *BMC Pregnancy Childbirth, 17*, 283.

Laney, E., Hall, M., Anderson, T., & Willingham, M. (2015). Becoming a mother: The influence of motherhood on women's identity development. *Identity, 15*, 126–145.

LaSusa. (2021). Existential crisis of motherhood. *The New York Times.*

Lau, E. Y. H., Li, J.-B., & Siu, C. T.-S. (2022). Postnatal depressive symptoms mediate the relation between prenatal role overload and responsiveness among first-time mothers. *Journal of Reproductive and Infant Psychology, 42*(1), 95–109.

Leder, D. (1990). *The absent body.* University of Chicago Press.

Leder, D. (2021). Healing time: The experience of body and temporality when coping with illness and incapacity. *Medicine, Health Care and Philosophy, 24*(1), 99–111.

Lundgren, I., & Wahlberg, V. (1999). The experience of pregnancy: A hermeneutical/phenomenological study. *The Journal of Perinatal Education, 8*(3), 12–20.

MacMahon. (1995). *Engendering motherhood: Identity and self-transformation in women's lives.* The Guilford Press.

Mandai, M., Kaso, M., Takahashi, Y., & Nakayama, T. (2018). Loneliness among mothers raising children under the age of 3 years and predictors with special reference to the use of SNS: A community-based cross-sectional study. *BMC Women's Health, 18*, 131.

Marinopoulos, S. (2005). *Nell'Intimo delle Madri.* Feltrinelli.

Merleau-Ponty, M. (1945). *Phenomenology of perception.* Routledge.

Mir, S. (2022). The pain of parental impostor syndrome. *The Guardian.*

Oakley, A. (1984). *The captured womb: A history of the medical care of pregnant women.* Blackwell.

Oatridge, A., Holdcroft, A., Saeed, N., Hajnal, J. V., Puri, B. K., Fusi, L., & Bydder, G. M. (2002). Change in brain size during and after pregnancy: Study in healthy women and women with preeclampsia. *AJNR. American Journal of Neuroradiology, 23*(1), 19–26.

Osler, L. (2021). (Un) wanted feelings in anorexia nervosa: Making the visceral body mine again. *Philosophy, Psychiatry, & Psychology, 28*(1), 67–69.

Pinkola Estés, C. (1995). *Women who run with the wolves.* Random House Publishing Group.

Prizeman, K., Weinstein, N., & McCabe, C. (2023). Effects of mental health stigma on loneliness, social isolation, and relationships in young people with depression symptoms. *BMC Psychiatry, 23*(1), 527.

Roberts. (2023). Women killed by sons. *The Guardian.*

Sacks, A. (2017). The birth of a mother. *The New York Times.*

Stern, D. N., Bruschweiler-Stern, N., & Freeland, A. (1998). *The birth of a mother: How the motherhood experience changes you forever.* Basic Books.

Taylor, B. L., Howard, L. M., Jackson, K., Johnson, S., Mantovani, N., Nath, S., Sokolova, A. Y., & Sweeney, A. (2021). Mums alone: Exploring the role of isolation and loneliness in the narratives of women diagnosed with perinatal depression. *Journal of Clinical Medicine, 10*(11), 2271.

Thompson, L., Rickett, B., & Day, K. (2018). Feminist relational discourse analysis: Putting the personal in the political in feminist research. *Qualitative Research in Psychology, 15*(1), 93–115.

Trifu, S., Vladuti, A., & Popescu, A. (2019). The neuroendocrinological aspects of pregnancy and postpartum depression. *Acta Endocrinologica (Bucharest, Romania: 2005), 15*(3), 410–415.

Van der Kolk, B. (2015). *The body keeps the score.* Penguin Publisher.

Wekesa, E., Askew, I., & Abuya, T. (2018). Ambivalence in pregnancy intentions: The effect of quality of care and context among a cohort of women attending family planning clinics in Kenya. *PLoS One, 13*(1), e0190473.

INDEX

For Product Safety Concerns and Information please
representative GPSR@taylorandfrancis.com Taylor & F
Kaufingerstraße 24, 80331 München, Ger

Printed by Printforce, the Netherland